IDEAS IN
PRACTICE

THE LONDON CENTRE FOR PSYCHOTHERAPY

PRACTICE OF PSYCHOTHERAPY SERIES

Series Editors
*Bernardine Bishop, Angela Foster,
Josephine Klein, Victoria O'Connell*

PRACTICE OF PSYCHOTHERAPY SERIES

BOOK TWO

IDEAS IN
PRACTICE

edited by

Bernardine Bishop, Angela Foster,
Josephine Klein, Victoria O'Connell

on behalf of

The London Centre for Psychotherapy

KARNAC

LONDON   NEW YORK

First published in 2002 by
H. Karnac (Books) Ltd.
6 Pembroke Buildings, London NW10 6RE

A subsidiary of Other Press LLC, New York

British Library Cataloguing in Publication Data

A C.I.P. for this book is available from the British Library

ISBN 1 85575 976 4

10 9 8 7 6 5 4 3 2 1

Edited, designed, and produced by The Studio Publishing Services Ltd,
Exeter EX4 8JN

Printed in Great Britain by Biddles Ltd., Guildford and King's Lynn

www.karnacbooks.com

CONTENTS

EDITORS AND CONTRIBUTORS

All contributors to this book are members of the London Centre for Psychotherapy

BERNARDINE BISHOP has a background in academic English, writing and teaching. She is a psychoanalytic psychotherapist in private practice in London.

PROPHECY COLES is a psychoanalytic psychotherapist. She trained at the Lincoln Centre for Psychotherapy. She is a training therapist for several institutions including the LCP. From the mid 80s until the late 90s she was co-chair of The Inner City (psychotherapy and counselling) Centre. She was for many years on the editorial board of the British Journal of Psychotherapy. She was on the founding Ethical committee of the BCP. Her most recent publication is a contribution to *Psychoanalysis and Psychotherapy: the Controversies and the Future* (Karnac Books, 2001).

LORRAINE COLLEDGE has a background in Health and Social Services. She currently combines working for a local authority with a private practice in psychoanalytic psychotherapy.

ANGELA FOSTER had a career in social worker and higher education before training as a psychotherapist. She is a psychoanalytic psychotherapist in private practice and a partner in Foster Roberts Cardona through which she provides organisational consultancy and professional development services. She has published widely in the field of mental health and is co-editor of and a principal contributor to *Managing Mental Health in the Community: chaos and containment* (A. Foster & V. Roberts (Eds.), Routledge, 1898).

JOSEPHINE KLEIN was an academic for the first twenty years of her professional life and then a psychoanalytic psychotherapist in private practice, now retired. Her two most recent publications are *Our Need for Others and its Roots in Infancy*. Routledge, previously Tavistock 1987 and *Doubts and Uncertainties in the Practice of Psychotherapy* (Karnac Books, 1995).

VIVIENNE LEWIN is a psychoanalytic psychotherapist in private practice. She has previously published "Working with a Twin: Implications for the transference". *British Journal of Psychotherapy*, 10(4), 1994.

VICTORIA O'CONNELL comes from a background of work with children with emotional difficulties. She is now a psychoanalytic psychotherapist in private practice.

ROBERT ROYSTON is a psychoanalytic psychotherapist in private practice. He has published papers on cognitive inhibition, narcissistic deprivation, sexuality and other subjects. He worked formerly as a journalist and publisher.

JENNIFER SILVERSTONE is a training therapist and supervisor. In the recent past she has written on Benjamin Wilkormirski and is interested in truth and fiction and its relationship to literature and psychoanalysis.

The London Centre for Psychotherapy

The London Centre for Psychotherapy has its origins in the 1950s and became a registered charity in 1974. Its activities are threefold:

- To offer training in psychoanalytic psychotherapy (including analytical psychology) in which the leading schools of analytic thought and practice are represented.
- To organise post-graduate professional activities and;
- To provide a psychotherapy service to the community through its clinic.

The Centre is the professional association of around 200 practising psychotherapists who are registered, through the Centre, with the British Confederation of Psychotherapists.

The LCP

32 Leighton Road • Kentish Town • London NW5 2QE
Telephone: 020 7482 2002/2282 • Fax: 020 74782 4222

www.lcp-psychotherapy.org.uk

Registered Charity No. 267244

Introduction

This is the second volume in the series *The Practice of Psychotherapy* by members of the London Centre for Psychotherapy.

We have brought these six contributions together under the title *Ideas in Practice*. This needs a little explanation. We believe that in each of these papers there is the spark of an original idea, an idea very much of the author's own, grounded indeed in psychoanalytic theory, but influenced by individual experience and observation in the consulting room. This could be a description of any clinical paper. But, without making special claims, in the juxtaposition of the words "ideas" and "practice", we have found a common resonance in these very different papers. All show working psychotherapists trying to learn from their patients and from themselves, and arriving at a formulation that seems to offer a rather personal perspective and a little bit of light.

Vivienne Lewin and Prophecy Coles have as their focus the importance in psychic reality for some patients of early relationships with siblings. Vivienne Lewin presents experiences from working with twins, and thinks about the particular character that twin-ship is likely to stamp on later struggles for separateness.

1

Prophecy Coles considers how relationships with siblings, rather than with parents, may be the decisive factor in the internal worlds of some patients. Both authors have discovered the hard way that unless these complexities are firmly grasped by the therapist the nature of the transference and countertransference may be misunderstood.

Lorraine Colledge and Robert Royston describe cases where pathological structures cause stalemate in the movement of transference and countertransference until the therapist's radical shift of mind and heart creates a new situation, and, for the patients, establishes the therapist as a new experience. When the therapist is able to become more conscious of and at more ease with how he/she is enlisted as an archaic object, he/she can become a volunteer rather than a conscript, and can begin to create a benign environment for radical change.

Bernardine Bishop and Jennifer Silverstone are concerned with the dire effects on personality development of maternal absence. In Bernardine Bishop's paper the mother's absence is physical, and what is being described is the effect of this sort of disruption on the growth of the very capacity to think. In Jennifer Silverstone's paper the absence is mostly of mind, and she links consequent narcissistic problems to confusion about the real meaning of the body within a self. The patients under discussion in these two papers have an urgent need to be reclaimed and harboured in a maternal mind. But they have adapted parts of the immature self to substitute for the unavailable objects and containers. The effects of this profound but often well-disguised damage can make the transference difficult to decipher.

We hope these ideas may be useful in practice.

CHAPTER ONE

The twin in the transference

Vivienne Lewin

T his paper is about twins and twinning, the impact on psychoanalytic work of the existence of an actual twin, and defensive twin-ship.

The primary emotional task facing an infant is the development of a sense of self, a personal identity, separate from but connected to mother and father. The task is complicated by the presence of a twin, whether mono- or di-zygotic, same or different sex. The twin-ship is an additional relationship to be dealt with by all members of the family, but most particularly by the twins themselves. They face a unique series of conflicts between remaining enmeshed and separating: a conflict within each individual twin, between the twins, and between them and their parents. The establishment of separateness from a twin is a process requiring parental help that takes place while the twins are working out their relationships with each parent and with the parental couple.

I have worked individually with a number of adult patients who have a twin, and therefore with the implications of twin-ship for the transference relationship. In working with the individual twin, the twin transference must be addressed in addition to the maternal and paternal object relationships, and the relationship to the parental couple as the creative couple. The twin-ship may be used as a defence by the patient and may make working through the oedipal situation more difficult. If the twin in the transference is not recognized and analysed, a fundamental aspect of the personality will remain inadequately known and integrated, and development towards separateness in the analysis will be impeded.

A twin shares its mother with the other baby from the beginning of its life, even before birth, though is not clear at which stage of development one foetus becomes consciously aware of the other. Neither baby can ever be alone with mother and each twin is always shadowed by the other.

> The baby at the breast excludes the other both from mother and from itself and, while this might lead to feelings of triumph, it will also engender a fear of attack by the other excluded, envious baby. The baby at the breast will also have been the baby excluded at another time and will identify with the excluded baby, with its feelings of rage and rejection. [Lewin, 1994, p. 499]

However, the excluded twin may also identify with the satisfaction of the infant at the breast, and this together with mother's empathic awareness of the waiting infant may enable it to endure the wait more happily.

In the ordinary process of development, each twin faces a conflict between the twin-ship, with its lack of true containment provided by the other immature baby, and the relationship with mother, a mature container (Bion, 1962a) but one which interferes in the twin-ship. When the mother is the primary object, her maturity and capacity to transform unbearable anxieties into something more benign that can be introjected and integrated, enables the baby to grow and develop.

However, with twins, it is as if the psychic splitting processes have become embodied, leading to difficulty in establishing an identity separate from the twin:

> where the twin is the primary object, the projective and introjective identifications between the two set up powerful interpenetrating forces, creating a confusion of identities that is not adequately resolved by such processing, because neither twin has yet developed the capacity to do so. As a result, the twins create an interlocked state of arrested development where relating depends

on projective and introjective identification with the twin, based on splitting. There is a lack of individual ego boundaries and integrity, the "skin" being around the pair rather than the individual. [Lewin, 1994, p. 501]

The great ambivalence twins face in separating is illustrated by the following example.

A psychoanalyst referred to me a woman whose twin sister was in treatment with him. Both women were married, leading individual lives, but they thought there were issues to be resolved between them before they could feel more separate. The patient said she wanted to see me at a specific time on a specific day of the week—to coincide exactly with the time and day on which her twin had her session! When I was unable to offer this, she sought a psychotherapist who could.

The transference relationship

Twins often swing between two processes in an attempt to establish an untroubled twin-ship and to avoid separateness. On the one hand, they may try to establish sameness by denial of difference. Sameness represents an apparently conflict-free state, an illusion of absolute control, and the elimination of rivalry with possible victory for one and consequent humiliation for the other. On the other hand, they may create difference based on splitting and projection, to be rid of unwanted parts of the self, each twin representing different aspects of the twin-ship.

The struggle between twins may be a potent force in the transference relationship. The patient may attempt to create a twinship with the analyst by denial of difference, especially of generations, or may use projective identification to evacuate the more disturbing aspects of the self. The split off and disowned projections may then be viciously attacked in what seems to the patient to be a fierce battle between the twin in the analyst, and the patient. Interpretations may be felt by the patient as attempts by the analyst to be rid of these unwanted aspects and to force them back into the patient. The establishment of true difference and discrete ego boundaries by working through the processes of separateness and separation (Quinodoz, 1993) will be a major task in the analytic work.

The issue of separateness is, of course, not unique to twins and will be encountered in any psychoanalytic situation. Working with a twin is different, however, in that the transference will, in addition, represent the enmeshed twin relationship consisting of a confusion of aspects of the patient, plus introjected aspects of the actual twin. The possible transference relationships involved are with the actual twin, with the mother as the primary object, with the father as the secondary object, and with the combined parental couple. There is also the recognition of the other twin as different from the self, and in a relationship with both mother and father, and with the parental couple. The awareness of the other twin's experience of oneself in relation to the parents, as well as to itself, is a further aspect to be recognized. This complex transference twin needs careful exploration and interpretation to enable the patient to be extricated from the twin-ship towards a transference relationship based on a parental object.

Twinning is not limited to actual twins, but may also be used by a singleton through the creation of an imaginary twin. In the transference, the imaginary twin may be used in a search for greater understanding, by splitting off and projecting unknown parts of the self, as in the early infant/mother relationship. Or it may be defensively used to avoid knowing these split off parts of the self. It may also be used for the splitting off known and unwanted aspects of the self that are then projected into the transference twin. Twinning, either as a defence or in a search for greater knowledge, has to be dealt with before the patient can re-integrate the split-off parts of the self, which have been located in the imaginary twin.

There is a "... common fantasy that any one of us might have a clone, a doppelganger, someone who is not only a human mirror but also an ideal companion; someone who understands me perfectly, almost perfectly, because he is me, almost me" (Wright, 1997, p. 33).

Klein (1963) addresses the issue when she writes of the common phantasy of having a twin in order to try to deal with loneliness. She suggests that this internal loneliness is a result of "... a ubiquitous yearning for an unattainable perfect internal state" (p. 300). The "... unsatisfied longing for an understanding without words"

(p. 300) derives from the good early relationship between mother and baby, when there is close contact between the unconscious of the mother and that of the child. "... the universal phantasy of having a twin ... represents those un-understood and split-off parts, which the individual is longing to regain, in the hope of achieving wholeness and complete understanding; they are sometimes felt to be ideal parts. At other times, the twin represents an entirely reliable, in fact, idealised internal object" (p. 302).

Wishing for a twin is a narcissistic affair, a defence that brings the narcissistic mirroring closer. Britton (2000) describes a narcissistic state that is not simply a withdrawal from external objects to an internal object. It is a particular kind of internal object relationship in which the separate existence and particular qualities of the internal object are denied and an internal narcissistic relationship is created by projective identification. An internal twinning is set up between the self and the ego ideal, denying the ego's need for love from the super-ego. "Twin internal souls united by a narcissistic love" (p. 3). Such a narcissistic relationship, where the superego is evaded, is realized externally in a relationship with an idealized twin.

The narcissistic patient builds up a phantasy of an omnipotent self and an omnipotently created object (a twin); the analyst is regarded as a threat to this relationship. Such patients have difficulty establishing an ordinary transference relationship with the analyst, either remaining aloof and detached, or "... adherent, clamorous and concrete in their transference attachment but in neither situation is the analyst experienced as both significant and separate" (Britton, 2000, p. 2).

Bion (1967a) describes the defensive emergence of an imaginary twin in the transference, to cover up and avoid meeting an un-understood part of the self. On recognizing and interpreting the twinning rhythm set up by the patient, access to the Oedipus complex was unblocked, as was the patient's ability to think. With the emergence of the imaginary twin in the transference, the patient changed from using the processes of splitting and personification to disown a bad part of himself from which he wished to be dissociated, to a recognition of the analyst as a non-identical twin i.e. as separate, a person in his own right, not just a thing created by him.

Bion notes that prior to this recognition, his interpretations generated immense anxiety in the patient, not only from the content of the associations, but because he was drawing attention to the intra-psychic processes.

He explains that:

> the imaginary twin goes back to his very earliest relationship and is an expression of his inability to tolerate an object that was not entirely under his control. The function of the imaginary twin was thus to deny a reality different from himself. With this denial of external reality, there co-existed his inability to tolerate the internal psychic realities and a great deal of work had to be done before any increase in tolerance occurred. [Bion, 1967a, p. 19]

In actual twins, there may be collusion between them to confirm a permanent identity, in order to cover up rivalry and difference. The idea that twins are "identical" is a defence against acknowledging difference. Many studies concentrate on the identicalness of twins and extraordinary similarities have been observed, e.g. in their movements, mannerisms, and even life events. Studies on twins separated at birth and re-united as adults are quite startling in the convergence demonstrated (Wright, 1998). The biological/genetic dimension of physical and psychological identity in twins is a factor, but even monozygotic twins differ both emotionally and physically.

As Bion's describes, it may take time for the twin relationship to emerge into the transference. The twin-ship, its specific nature in each patient, including the difference between an actual and an imaginary twin-ship, is at this time, at the core of the work to be addressed. Until it emerges in the transference, is recognized and analysed, progress towards the establishment of separateness through the transference experience of a parental relationship with the analyst is limited. When the patient leaves treatment before this has happened, there is a sense of lack of resolution and unsatisfactory outcome, as shown by the following example.

A small robust middle-aged woman, with a twin brother, sought help because she had difficulties with relationships in a number of areas of her life, but she regarded her main problem as her mother. She experienced mother as possessive, intrusive, dominating and demanding. While father was regarded as more distant and unimportant, mother was seen as powerful, well educated and a high achiever. Identifying with mother, the patient saw herself as the source of power and resources, and felt those around her, including her mother, flocked to her for help. Her twin brother, in contrast, was seen as always sick, weak, and in need of her protection. She felt she had always to look after him, to rescue him from difficult situations, and although she hated the forced intimacy and sharing, she felt she could never rid herself of her brother, as they were never allowed to be separate.

The patient felt rather guilty about her twin, as she was the healthier baby at birth; her twin was substantially underweight. She felt she had taken more sustenance than was her due. At birth, when her twin was put in an incubator, the patient was placed alongside him to help him in his struggle for survival. As a child when she heard her asthmatic brother struggle for breath, she thought (wished and feared) he would die. With her feelings of both guilt and fierce resentment she felt painfully entangled with her twin. It is as if only one of the twins can survive, while the other is half-dead.

Her experience of being in the incubator with her twin would be an unconscious one enriched by parental comment, a birth narrative. It also represents the relationship with the mother—an incubator mother, hard, impenetrable and intrusive, a high-achiever mother making enormous demands on her. While longing for a non-demanding, non-intrusive mother, she identified with the incubator mother and colluded with achiever-mother to denigrate warm soft mothering that tolerates vulnerability, both of them being contemptuous of the weaker twin brother.

She felt she gave too much of herself, was experienced as overwhelming, but not receiving much in return. In contrast her twin was a pale needy figure. She saw him as a split off bad self that tormented her, containing the buried feelings of which she was so afraid, the hated needy twin self. This needy twin was an ever - present shadow, torturing her with his existence.

As I listened to her angry outpourings, I found myself feeling dominated and rather helpless (no doubt like her twin). She seemed to have a clear view of herself and little interest in anything I might have to say. It was as if I was the twin in the incubator whom she had to look after. When I did intervene, she felt I was like her intrusive dominating incubator-mother. When I interpreted this, she understood this as confirmation that I was indeed behaving like her mother. She found it intolerable that I might be able to provide insight that she lacked, all the while complaining that she never found any of her relationships, including that with me, rewarding.

As she became more aware of her relatedness to me as someone who could think separately and whom she did not control, she started missing sessions, and then left precipitately, without again making contact. As long as I accepted being the helpless twin whom she would look after, she tolerated me. But with evidence of my separateness, she abandoned me, as she wished to do with her twin. I was the one to be left high and dry while she made off with all the resources. She was unwilling to tolerate owning a needy-twin aspect of herself, helped by a productive mother.

Defensive twinning and symbolization

The successful working through of the complex issues of need and dependency in relation to a mature container, the acknowledgement of difference and the envy and rage this stirs, and all aspects of separateness and separation, will depend on the capacities of the patient to use symbolic thinking. At times of difficulty, the patient will frequently regress to former patterns of coping—the twin relationship.

Both patients Bion (1967a) describes use the twin transference defensively. Patient A initially uses an imaginary twin to alleviate anxiety by preventing the birth in the analyst of someone who is different and separate, and has freedom of thought. The patient has created a relationship much like that with an enmeshed actual twin. When this is interpreted, the patient is able to use this personification of the split-off portions of his personality for reality testing, like play therapy. He is able to use the twin material for phantasy, to symbolize. However, patient B, who has an actual twin, remains unable to phantasize about the material of the imaginary twin, and he is unable to develop insight about his psychic processes. We don't really know why his ability to symbolize is so limited, though Bion describes him as a more disturbed personality. In this paper, however, Bion does not explore the difference in the transference twin where an actual twin exists or how it will affect the twin transference.

As Bion describes it, the movement from using the processes of splitting and personification to deny the existence of an object not directly under his control and to deny a reality different from himself, to the use of these processes to make contact with an outer reality, represents a move from a twinning relationship towards a parental one. The development of insight through the analysis increases the investigative capacities of the patient and this reactivates emotions associated with early advances in psychological development. For patient A, this was a relationship between father and child. "With 'A', the change from a perfunctory and superficial treatment of the Oedipus situation to a struggle to come to terms with an emotionally charged Oedipus complex was extremely striking" (p. 21). Patient B, however, on encountering another patient, showed some development in becoming aware of a "...by no means identical twin that had a relationship with a mother" (p. 21), but was unable to use this material symbolically, and Bion still remained only an identical twin to him.

Kohut (1984) distinguishes between normal and pathological twinning in the transference. He regards normal twin-ship as a need based on the experience of the presence of essential likeness, the self-affirming and self-maintaining experiences of early childhood that are important in enabling us to feel human amongst humans, to have a sense of belonging and of participating. He regards pathological twinning in the transference as an attempt to repair structures that were damaged early in life, as in borderline patients. He describes a patient who told him shortly before a break, that from the age of 6 years, she had kept a stoppered bottle in which she imagined a person living, a little girl, a twin, someone like herself but not herself, someone sufficiently like her to understand her—an imaginary twin created by her to compensate for unbearable loss and loneliness.

The creation in the transference of an imaginary twin that is used to exclude a maternal object is, I think, akin to a borderline state (Steiner, 1993). The imaginary twin represents a psychic retreat from the development towards the depressive position, and is used to avoid the pain of relinquishing phantasies of omnipotent control, and of loss of the illusion of possession of the good object.

Movement away from the twin as the primary object, towards the separate maternal primary object, depends on the recognition of the primary object as one not like self. Tolerating this move involves recognition of the "supremely good breast" (Money-Kyrle, 1971) as the primary object and understanding that, in contrast, both twins are in the same position and face the same predicament. For each, the good breast is shared not only with the other twin, but also with father and all siblings. Neither of the twins is or possesses this good breast. The recognition of the parental couple, and not the twin couple, as the "supremely creative couple" (Money-Kyrle, 1971), is also necessary to disentangle the twin relationship. Where this three-person relationship can be established for each twin, boundaried by the relationship between the parents, an internal space is created, a third position, a capacity for observing and being observed, i.e. for thinking (Britton, 1989).

Rivalry in twins

There is always rivalry in twins and any apparent non-rivalry is a powerful defence and should arouse suspicion (see Engel below). Where twins are enmeshed and a maternal object does not sufficiently mediate the intense rivalry between them, the only possible resolution is via triumph and vanquishment—of one over the other. In this situation, the rivalry is not predominantly for the attention of mother, but for the omnipotent possession of the (pseudo-) breast. Where a maternal object is recognized, there is rivalry for the dominant position and possession of mother. The sibling rivalry is increased because of the special nature of the twin relationship.

If the mother has the capacity, and if the twins have the capacity and will allow her intervention, a place can be created for each infant to grow and develop with tolerance of the other and of the maternal relationship with the twin, and with father. Mediating in this way and with love for each infant in its own right allows movement towards the depressive position and greater maturity. But it may be that either the mother, or the twins, or one twin more than the other, has a limited capacity for such development and then the twins may remain enmeshed.

The Gibbons twins (Wallace, 1996), are an example of the most damaging sort of development.

"Identical" twins, June and Jennifer grew up in an apparently caring and communicative family, but kept themselves isolated from their parents and siblings. From childhood, they shared a secret language and spoke only to one another, and to a younger sister. At school they remained frozen in their silence. As teenagers, they became even more reclusive. "Ever since they left school … they had shut themselves away in their bunk bedroom, never coming down to meals, never even smiling at other members of the family or acknowledging their presence in the house" (p. 2).

The twins would sometimes dress up and go out together. They exhibited rather bizarre and delinquent behaviour and at 17, were jailed for repeated arson and theft. In jail they were separated.

Wallace describes her first interview with June, in prison:

> I could see June's eyes flickering and her mouth edging into something resembling a smile. But her words were torn whispers, her whole being was strung between a desperate need to speak and some destructive internal command which forbade her such freedom. She would start to tell me something, then suddenly gag as though an invisible presence had put its hands around her throat. Who or what could hold such power over a human being, to compel her to lifelong silence and immobility? What inner force gave her the strength to reject everything and everyone offering help or affection? What had happened to allow a potentially attractive young girl to waste her youth, not just behind the walls of a prison but behind her own private defences? [p. 5]

A poem by June describes her mortal entanglement with Jennifer:

> Without my shadow would I die?
> Without my shadow would I gain life?
> Be free or left to die? [p. 255]

In 1993, as they were released from Broadmoor and just reconciled, Jennifer suddenly died. Wallace tells of June dictating a poem to the dead Jennifer, describing how

> ...like a blind Delius to her Emanuensis,
> [she] spoke, staring into space.
> Like the closing of an autumn door,
> another door opens.
> Somewhere in the deep dark room,
> an old wound has reopened.
> Somewhere in this muddled world,
> a tiny child is crying,
> reaching out to hold its heart.
> The wind dies, then it starts.
> When I look up to the sky,
> I see the aftermath within your eye.
> You left me stone-cold and broken
> and I never asked you why. [p. 272]

Jennifer's death was sudden and mysterious. She died of acute myocarditis, but such a sudden onset and deterioration is apparently unusual. She had binged and starved herself for many years in her rivalry with June. Perhaps she had weakened her immune defences so drastically that she "...succumbed with all the resistance of a sacrificial lamb" (p. 274). Wallace speculates about whether there was a pact between them "...that June, the first born, the stronger, would finally gain her birthright" (p. 274).

Wallace wonders what will happen to June: "When the first flush and relief of her loss fades, will she find life without her shadow intolerable? Or will she find that without her 'dark sister robbing her of her sunlight' she can enter a new era of her life, carrying Jennifer with her, confident that she, June can live for both of them" (p. 274).

June wanted a banner to fly in the sky on the 1st anniversary of Jennifer's death, to read, "June is fine, she is fit and well and her own person. She has come into her own" (p. 273). She told Wallace, "At long last I am all June, not a part of Jennifer. Somebody had to break the vicious circle. We were war weary. It had been a long battle. We were both a burden to each other" (p. 273).

The twin-ship myth of shared identity

Where there is insufficient separation of the twins, neither develops a clear sense of personal identity. In this situation so much of the "self" is split off and lodged in the other, that each is uncertain what belongs where, and who is who.

A woman patient with an "identical" twin felt she had no identity separate from her twin. She was the second born, and was regarded as a "total shock", not a lovely surprise, from which the parents never recovered. The parents were experienced as denying the separate existence of the second twin, dressing both twins exactly alike, insisting on absolute equality between them even if this meant depriving one of them of a hard-won scholarship. They were seen as two halves of one whole. Both twins were usually referred to by the name of the older one, and the younger one was regarded as the shadow or reflection of the other. Unlike her twin, my patient was not named for some time after birth, as her parents thought she might die. She felt as if she were like a charcoal and chalk portrait that could be rubbed out.

She was told she suffered from projectile vomiting as an infant, and was apparently fed in a room covered in plastic sheeting and with all carpets removed. A more bleak and unloving scenario would be hard to describe, and one that suggests particular difficulties with projective and introjective processes, as if they were felt to be violent experiences. This is not too surprising for an unexpected and apparently unwanted baby denied a separate existence from her twin. With such seemingly forbidding and denying parents who had little compassion for her, her only developmental refuge was her twin.

While I felt very moved by her story, she experienced me as cold and ungiving. She appeared to be bound up with her twin, to be smug and self-contained. She seemed to have no real communication with me but to be excluding me and talking to herself. Her primary relationship was with her twin and she did not hold me in mind nor believe I did her. She regarded sessions as seamless, held together by a thread and without any gap, as if I did not live a separate life from her. After the start of each session, I had to intervene in this imaginary twin-ship to establish my separate existence.

She described her relationship with her sister as "almost like Siamese twins" .She believed her twin was the loved child with all the good memories. She also, however, felt her twin was an intolerable burden, the carrier of her unwanted feelings and she wished her twin were dead, thinking that was the only way to be rid of her. She thought that her sister handled her all over and experienced her twin as trying to get right inside her like a parasite, and that she had to get her out of her. She believed I would invade her also and distanced herself from me. She hated mirrors, as the reflection seemed to be her twin, the preferred child with all the good memories, and the hated parasite.

As children the twins had a private language, and as adults there were still secret ways in which they communicated. The wish for secret and perfect communication was reflected in the therapy by her frequent demands that I should explain to her what I had understood of what she had said, as if to prove that like a twin, my understanding of her was complete. She was angry with me for using my words, not hers, as it meant we were not identical twins.

As children they fought violently and were mutually filled with both hatred of each other and a fear of separating that felt like being torn apart. Some years before my patient entered therapy, her twin had become disabled and extremely disturbed emotionally. My patient became obsessed with her hatred of her twin, but was burdened with keeping her twin alive through several attempted suicides, and against the expressed wish of her sister to die. Her twin became extremely demanding, leading my patient to feel desperate in her wish to be separate, although she believed her twin would not survive alone. This belief was reflected in our work where she felt I denied changes in her as if I was a twin unable to bear her growth and development away from me.

As her sister's health declined, my patient gained in strength, as if magically robbing her sister of her vitality. With the development of greater understanding of herself, she reported feeling noticeably different outside sessions. She became more reflective and separate from her sister and realized she was not responsible for her sister's illness. This understanding led to a temporary fear of freedom and backsliding in the work. With the development of some feelings of separateness, she felt she had got her sister out of her, and this led to feelings of both emptiness and relief. She could see how intertwined she and her twin had been and recognize the basis of her fears of madness.

Towards the end of the therapy, it became apparent that both father and her twin sister had bullied her as a child and that it felt safer to be her sister's shadow and therefore not really seen and punished. She sometimes felt she had brought her sister into the consulting room with her and that she could not speak freely, because there were things she had never told her twin and she would be punished for this. The twin-ship represented both power and anonymity.

As her sense of a separate identity increased, the patient described how she had seen a video of herself and could see for the first time ever that she was different from her twin. Her twin kept asking her if they were the same, and when my patient said no, the sister expressed her fear that she was losing her twin and clung to the twin-ship. Others saw the changes in her, and her twin told her she was horrible. My patient then became afraid that I would not allow her to leave the therapy when she was ready or that I would end the therapy prematurely.

Although the twin-ship resurfaced as the ending approached, with her insistence that I knew what she thought without her having to tell me, and wanting to get right inside my mind, she was able to tolerate the loss of the illusion of possession of me, to see my separateness, and her loss of me in parting. She emerged as a sexual woman with her own thoughts and feelings and relationships. She felt the world had opportunities for her.

She recognized that for much of the therapy she had brought with her the burden of another, her twin sister, and now that they were separate she could see her twin as childish in her vulnerability, fearsome in her anger, but not part of her. She was also able to stand up to her formerly terrifying parents and be different and say she was. She felt she could respect their difference and saw them as less persecutory. With her separateness from me, she welcomed the fluidity of her thoughts.

This work does raise issues about working with one twin only and the effect on the other, as described by Sheerin (1991). My patient's twin was clearly a very ill woman. The separation as a result of my work with the patient exposed the illness even more clearly. Did it also exacerbate it?

The idea that twins are "identical", as in the case above, and that the other is already known, as in the patient who is described

below, is based on a belief that the other is like me. Known parts of
the self are split off and attributed to the other. This twinning
defence leads to a cover-up and collusion, and unlike the situation
described by Melanie Klein regarding loneliness, is not based on the
splitting off of unknown parts with the hope of understanding and
recovery of those parts in a more familiar form. The common twin-
ship myth of a shared identity, the idea of identical personalities, is
a narcissistic way of framing the other like the self. One sees oneself
in the other in order to avoid something else, something different. It
is when there is a breakthrough to unknown material that difference
can be recognized and established.

> A middle-aged man with a twin brother thought, immediately on
> entering my consulting room for the first time, that he had met me
> before, i.e. that he already knew me. This twin transference was
> evidence of an entangled twin-ship projected into me. His wife also
> served as his emotional twin, and like his twin brother, she
> expressed feelings for him.

> His twin had required surgery immediately after birth and with
> mother's attention to his twin, the patient felt that mother had
> robbed him of his twin by separating them and leaving him in the
> care of father. He felt he was always the bad twin, never able to do
> right, while his twin was the good one, much favoured especially by
> mother. But he always had to look after his twin, rescue him from
> fights at school. He believed he had to speak for his twin from a very
> early age, partly because of the surgery the twin had undergone, but
> also because they were so entwined it was as if they shared a
> personality. In turn, he used his twin to get what he wanted from
> mother.

> He felt mother was dominating and attacking and if I said anything
> that touched his feelings, he likewise experienced me as a
> persecuting mother. He was able to recognize that he placed his
> twin between him and me; that he created an imaginary twin in me
> with whom he communicated, and that if I intervened in this with
> an interpretation, I became the mother who separated him from his
> twin, thus robbing him of those parts of himself carried by his twin.
> He felt he needed my exclusive attention as a twin and became very
> angry if he did not get it. It left him feeling as if he did not fully exist.

The twin relationship, birth narratives, and death

Each twin I have worked with has an individual story of birth that reflects a perceived relationship with the twin, but common themes emerge. The sense of being enmeshed has been described, for example, as the twins being interlocked at birth; intense and murderous rivalry as one twin being left aside as dead. It is common to feel that one baby has taken too much, with the result that the other twin was deprived of life-giving sustenance and has been sickly ever since. How much more disabling, then, when one twin dies at birth while the other has a good birth weight.

When a twin dies, the omnipotent control of the phantasied and remembered dead twin is unchecked by opposition of a live twin, or by the intervention of the mother in the twin-ship, as she may be quite unaware of the infant's memories of its twin. The shift to the acceptance of a maternal container, rather than the dead twin self in a psychic retreat is therefore more intense and difficult. Not only has the survivor not been freed from a possibly difficult twin-ship, but an additional burden has been added in that the dead twin carries, in the phantasies of the survivor, very powerful projections linked with life and death, survival and revenge. These become active in the transference. The complexity and conflict of feelings generated by this situation make it especially sensitive and difficult to resolve, and will play an important part in the ending of the analytic work.

For enmeshed twins bound in a rigid structure of intense rivalry, to relinquish omnipotent control of the other in a developmental move, will expose feelings of vulnerability, and unleash fear of attack and annihilation by the other twin, seeking revenge. Where one twin has died, the phantasied twin carries such intense projections that its imagined revenge will seem even greater.

The pattern of relating observed between twins *in utero* may persist after birth (Piontelli, 1992). Where one twin dies, the surviving baby will experience the absence of its twin and a profound feeling of loss. The parental reaction to the surviving baby is likely to be mixed. The birth is not only an event to be celebrated; it is also laden with loss and mourning. The surviving baby may seem more precious to the parents, but there is also ample scope for idealization of the dead baby and the consequent difficulty in accepting the survivor wholeheartedly.

The stories about the birth and death of the babies will influence the surviving twin's sense of acceptance or rejection by the parents, and its feelings of guilt and anxiety in relation to the death of its twin. The surviving baby can only deal in a very primitive way with the triumph of its survival and the loss of its twin, and it is greatly dependent on the parents for enabling it to emerge from this situation without feeling extremely persecuted and perhaps fragmented, in a situation inherently fraught with difficulty.

Steiner (1990) describes the difficulties faced by borderline patients in mourning their lost objects, their inability to relinquish control over objects and consequent failure to experience true separateness. The rigid organization created by binding the projected parts of the self with the object containing them in a complex structure, as in twins, requires gradual dismantling before the object can be recognized as separate, and relinquished and mourned. Guilt and mental pain have to be borne as disowned parts of the self are regained and the ego is enriched.

I referred earlier to Kohut's description of the creation of an imaginary twin to try and deal with loss (the twin in the stoppered bottle). Phantasies that the dead twin is still alive and present are common. Surviving twins have described the feeling that if only they could turn quickly enough to look behind them, they would see the dead twin, secretly still alive. Sometimes the surviving twin believes they are keeping the dead twin alive—and in a way they are, in phantasy.

There is commonly a belief that the surviving twin lives on for both of them, as described earlier in the Gibbons twins. Case (1993) quotes from a number of letters about the feelings generated by the death of a twin. One writes, "A major part of my life and of me was laid to rest when Kathy died. For 23 years one-half of me was her, and I think it always will be. Just as a part of me is gone, a part of Kathy lives on through me" (p. 18).

Some seek to maintain the twin-ship through spiritual union with the dead twin, in denial of loss. One year after the death of her twin, a woman writes:

Since Mary's death my whole world has become clouded. I have become overwhelmed with fears of isolation and abandonment. In a sense, I search for her. I surround myself with pictures, talk about her constantly, relive memories, and share every thought and prayer with her. Despite my efforts to survive, I feel that it is not natural to be physically separated from her. In fact is seems terribly wrong. I keep thinking, "I am going to die because Mary and I must always be together". I feel a separation from Mary that causes physical pains in my chest, On the other hand, I have never felt closer to her, as we are now joined by a spiritual bond which is unique to us. [p. 50]

A woman whose twin died *in utero* writes:

One moment, I can feel devastatingly lonely and not be able to wait for the day when I can die to go meet him in heaven. Just to hug him and tell him how much I love him. Yet at the same time I feel so incredibly guilty for being alive, like I don't deserve it... [p. 63]

Denial of the loss of the twin will be at great cost to personal identity. However, mourning may resolve this, with consequent enrichment of the life of the surviving twin.

A bereaved twin writes:

Seventeen years have passed. As long without Karen as with her. I now realise that I've been running instead of dealing with the pain of the loss. I stopped denying the loss and I'm able to be aware of my body, opinions and thoughts. I'm now developing a life that includes Karen as a fond memory. I'm not forsaking Karen, instead I'm honoring myself and the life I have to live. [p. 28]

Another discovers the value of separateness after the death of her twin:

And now? Finding oneself. Knowing one's capabilities. Finding sudden joy in knowing that I could attempt something: an assignment at work, writing poems, accomplishing a new weight-loss program, all without the twin-oriented dependence. Laughter coming easily (it never did before). A new person discovering capabilities and potential never known before. [p. 42]

The conjoined twins, "Jodie" and "Mary" have been much in the news recently and have stirred intense debate about the ethical and moral issues involved in separating them, as one twin would inevitably die as a result. Less has been expressed, however, about the emotional impact of the separation on the surviving twin. At a time when so much of the experience of the infants is somatically based, the effects of the loss of a conjoined twin must be profound, even when they both live. A documentary on the separation of another pair of conjoined twins showed how, immediately after coming round from the anaesthetic, one twin reached out for the other. When one twin dies in order to allow the other to live, the survivor will experience not only the guilt engendered by this situation, and parents deeply affected by it, but a profound sense of loss of part of the self, as well as of the twin.

Persistent issues in twin-ships

Even with effective psychoanalytic work that addresses the developmental processes faced by twins, the importance and depth of mutual identification can play a long-term role in the life of the patient. George Engel (1975) movingly describes the intensity of identification with a twin, and how this continues after the death of the twin (even in adulthood). His "identical" twin died of a heart attack at the age of 49. When, 11 months later, he too had a heart attack, his initial reaction was one of relief—he no longer had to anticipate a heart attack, "... the other shoe had fallen" (p. 25).

He used self-analysis of dreams and notes of events, particularly with regard to anniversary reactions to the death of his twin brother. With disarming honesty, he traces his development over those years with particular reference to the relationship with his twin. He suggests that one of the distinctive features of twinning is the "... pronounced tendency toward persistent confusion of identities in the unconscious" (p. 32).

He writes:

A central developmental issue for twins concerns the fact that separation and individuation must ultimately involve the twin as well as the mother. Indeed there is an indication that the intimacy and intensity of the interaction between the twins may actually accelerate the separation from the mother ... only to be replaced by a prolonged symbiosis between the twins whose separation and individuation from each other may be consequently long delayed. [p. 32]

This "twinning reaction" is based on diffuse ego-boundaries, on the one hand, and complementarity on the other, as a consequence of the prolonged struggle between unification and individuation of the twin pair. The twins develop complementary ego capacities to enhance the effective operation of the twin unit in relation to outsiders. Engel suggests that twins might exploit the narcissistic advantages of twin-ship precisely to avoid negotiating the Oedipus conflict.

He believes that three features may particularly affect the character of the grief response on the death of a twin, even after a degree of separation and independence has been achieved, as a result of the unique developmental features of twinning. These are "...the enduring diffuseness of the ego boundaries between self and object representations, the narcissistic gains of twin-ship, and the delicate balance of the defences against aggression" (p. 34) that have been developed between the twins.

Conclusion

Twinning in psychoanalytic work, with either a twin or a singleton, may be used either in the service of hoped for greater under-standing, or to avoid knowledge of aspects of the self, and of separateness and difference. If, as Engel describes, the nature of the response on the adult death of a twin is affected by the unique developmental aspects of twin-ship, even after a degree of separation and independence has been achieved, then it is clear that in any work with twins, the twin-ship in the transference must be recognized and worked through.

Only proper attention to the developmental processes faced by twins, including the unique and special nature of the relationship, can help twins to free themselves from the more primitive states of mind of an enmeshed twin-ship. Without sufficient intervention, twins cannot develop individually towards separateness and maturity, and may remain in an entwined identity capsule, a skin enclosing the pair. This will affect all their relationships, most notably those with a spouse or their children.

In analysis, if the twin-ship is not addressed, a core aspect of separateness will have been avoided and the ending will be un-satisfactory. When the twin transference is recognized and worked through, the patient can establish a sense of personal identity and be able to recognize the analyst as a separate person from whom he can take his leave with due mourning.

It may well be that through such work, both twins are helped in separating. But this may not be the case, and especially where there is a greater degree of disturbance, the situation of the twin not in treatment may be adversely affected by the development of the twin in treatment. This raises difficult issues about the psychoanalytic treatment of twins requiring careful thought.

CHAPTER TWO

The children in the apple tree: some thoughts on sibling attachment[1,2]

Prophecy Coles

I have been surprised to discover that little attention seems to have been given to siblings and to their role in psychic development, and very rarely in the literature is there a reference to a sibling transference. I am not the first to notice this. For instance, Ruth Lesser (1978) complained "No-one has written comprehensively on siblings as personae in the transference drama" (p. 39). Colonna and Newman (1983), in a survey on the psycho-analytic literature on siblings, wrote "We were amazed that we could not find a single paper dealing with siblings in the transference, though there were undoubtedly buried references to it in case reports" (p. 299). Ten years later it was still possible for Sharpe and Rosenblatt (1994) to write that "The nature of sibling relationships, in all their complex forms of love and hate, still remains more of a mystery than the passions and developmental vicissitudes of parent–child relationships" (p. 491). Why is that? The intuitive sense we all have is that if we have siblings they are very significant in our lives and if we do not, the absence is just as significant. Yet in the psychoanalytic literature they only feature as marginal and unwanted intruders.

One explanation might be that psychoanalytic thinking has been dominated by the Judaeo–Christian belief that siblings are rivals. This idea is strongly held in Western culture, with its myths of Cain and Abel, Jacob and Esau, Joseph and his brothers, and for the most part psychoanalytic theory has corroborated this belief. "The elder child ill-treats the younger, maligns him and robs him of his toys; while the younger is consumed with impotent rage against the elder, envies and fears him" (Freud, 1900, p. 250). Freud warned us not be deceived if we saw siblings becoming more loving and co-operative with each other for these feelings are always a reaction-formation to or reversal from the longed-for relationship with the parents (Freud, 1914, 1916–1917, 1923). The extent to which this view has tended to dominate psychoanalytic thinking is well conveyed in a summary by Freud and Dann (1951):

> The child's relationship to his brothers and sisters is subordinated to his relationship to the parents ... Siblings are normally accessories to the parents, the relations to them being governed by attitudes of rivalry, envy, jealousy and competition for the love of the parents. Aggression, which is inhibited toward the parents, is expressed freely toward brothers and sisters; sexual wishes, which cannot becomes manifest in the oedipal relationship, are lived, passively or actively, with the elder or younger brother and sisters. The under-lying relationship with siblings is thus a negative one ... with an overlay of positive feelings when siblings are used for the discharge of libidinal trends deflected from the parents. When relations among children of one family become finally manifestly positive, they do so according to the principles of group formation. [p. 166]

A further explanation may be to do with the claim that, because we all depend upon our parents in the first crucial years of attachment, siblings must necessarily be less important. This assertion can go on to incorporate the idea that siblings do not play a part in the internal world for they are out there and belong to "a 'real object' model only" (Graham, 1988, p. 88). This view relies upon a restricted view of the internal world in which only parental relationships are present.

There are, however, some authors who are persuaded of the importance for development of sibling relationships. They argue that siblings have been neglected in psychoanalytic theorizing because of a particular quality to the sibling transference. They suggest that the incest barrier between siblings does not have the same force as between parent and child. Sibling incest taboos develop from the matrix of childhood playing and exploration and the barrier against sexual enactment, at a young age, has a fluid quality. This is the transference that can find its way into therapy, and just because the prohibitions against enactment are less formidable, the sibling transference can arouse great anxiety in both patient and therapist. Rollman Branch (1966), Agger (1988), and Rudintsky (1987) believe that Freud feared to look at his own difficult feelings towards his siblings and as a result there has been an absence of recognition of the importance of siblings in development. Agger (1988) goes so far as to suggest that Freud's:

> formulation of the Oedipus Complex ... may have served a neurotic need for a cognitive vehicle to which ... (he) could attach a disturbing constellation of primitive feelings. To discover incestuous wishes and murderous fantasies toward parents may have been less distressing than to experience them in connection with siblings where the sadistic component and castration anxiety may have been more intense. [p. 12]

To suggest that at the core of Freud's theorizing of the Oedipal conflict lies a defensive construction against the more threatening conflict of sibling emotions is quite challenging. However, to see Freud's theory in this way interferes with the need to keep in view the essential differences between sibling and parental roles and relationships. We are necessarily dependent upon adults to take care of us and it is these earliest feelings of attachment, that are central to our emotional development. I do believe, nevertheless, that the understandable dominance of this view has obscured the separate and important meanings to be found in sibling relationships, and as a result these have not received the recognition they deserve.

Since the 1960s, and with the growth of Observation Studies on children, there has been an important shift in thinking about siblings and their relationships with each other, and a new awareness of the significance of sibling interactions (Brazelton, 1969; Parens, 1972, 1979; Lamb, 1978a,b; Lesser, 1978; Dunn & Kendrick, 1979; Bank & Kahn, 1997; Province & Solnit, 1983; Colonna & Newman, 1983; Kris & Ritvo, 1983; Neubauer, 1983;

Leichtman, 1985; Graham, 1988; Sharpe & Rosenblatt, 1994). These authors have observed the positive effect of sibling interactions and the way in which these interactions can facilitate growth and maturation. Envy, jealousy, and rivalry between siblings is seen as part of normal child development and not as the whole story (Neubauer, 1982). Children can have a meaningful relationship with an older sibling even during the first year of life (Parens, 1988). Older siblings can stand as models for younger siblings (Lamb, 1978a,b). Siblings can help each other separate from parents (Leichtman, 1985). Siblings can get pleasure and help from each other (Kris & Litvo, 1983). Sibling relationships have characteristics that are significantly different from parental relationships (Neubauer, 1983).

What these studies have also brought to light is the significance of birth order. It is true that Freud (1916) said "The position of a child in the family order is a factor of extreme importance in determining the shape of his later life" (p. 334). But, as the earlier quote shows, the emotions he suggested that siblings have for each other are aggression, on the part of the older, and impotent rage, on that of the younger. This view has tended to block further research on the effect of birth order on psychic development. Nevertheless there is increasing evidence from the authors quoted above that although an older sibling will feel rivalry, envy, and jealousy in the early months after the birth of a sibling, it is a mistake to imagine that the younger sibling begins his relations with an older brother or sister in a state of impotent rage. A younger sibling will never have known a world without siblings (Graham, 1988). Only at a later stage of development will the older siblings be envied. Therefore I agree with Leichtman (1985), who regards the sibling rivalry of the younger sibling as "superimposed on long-standing, largely positive attachments to and identifications with older siblings" (p. 147). Finally, what many of these studies are highlighting is the fact that siblings can play a significant part in the development of unconscious patterns of relating (Bank & Kahn, 1982). Kris & Ritvo (1983) go even further and assert that "a sibling relationship is always a factor in the choice of marital partner" (p. 322).

These studies on children over the last 30 years have helped to redress an imbalance and restore a commonsense knowledge that siblings hold a crucially important place in facilitating our attachment to the world, and that, in the rough and tumble of the nursery, we learn how to relate and live with our contemporaries (Colonna & Newman, 1983). We learn something else with our parents.

In an autobiographical moment, Freud (1900) acknowledged the importance of early attachments amongst children who live and play together. He had a nephew, John, Freud's half brother's son, who was 1 year older than Freud, and who lived next door to the Freud household. He said about John

> Until the end of my third year we had been inseparable; we had loved each other and fought each other, and ... this childhood relationship ... had a determining influence on all my subsequent relations with contemporaries. Since that time my nephew John has had many reincarnations which revived now one side and now another of his personality, unalterably fixed as it was in my unconscious memory ... All my friends have in a certain sense been reincarnations of the first figure ... they have been "revenants" ... My emotional life has always insisted that I should have an intimate friend and a hated enemy. I have always been able to provide myself afresh with both, and it has not infrequently happened that the ideal situation of childhood has been so completely reproduced that friend and enemy have come together in a single individual". [pp. 424, 483]

It is true that John was not Freud's brother, but nevertheless Freud's account does testify, in contrast to his theoretical formulations, to the importance and lasting influence of early attachments among children who grow up together. If Freud is intuitively right that all his later friends have been "reincarnations" of John, then it makes sense that these "revenants" may be found in adult relationships which people make. More importantly, we should not be surprised to find these "revenants" in our consulting room, nor should we be surprised to discover that in some cases these "revenants" are "ineradicably fixed" in the internal world of our patients.

It is puzzling that these early childhood relationships have been neglected in theory, when, at the same time, Freud and others, such as Melanie Klein, have suggested that they are so important. Melanie Klein (1975) was very sensitive to the importance of sibling relationships and went so far as to say:

> the existence of sexual relations between children in early life, especially between brothers and sisters, is a very common

occurrence. The libidinal craving of small children, intensified as it is by their Oedipus frustration, together with the anxiety emanating from their deepest danger-situations, impel them to indulge in mutual sexual activities, since these ... not only gratify their libido but enable them to search for manifold confirmations and refutations of their various fears in connection with the sexual act. I have repeatedly found that if such sexual objects have acted in addition as "helping figures", early sexual relations of this kind exert a favourable influence upon ... later sexual development ... (and can) ... provide the basis for a heterosexual position ... and develop ... (a) capacity for love. [p. 223]

As with the autobiographical passage quoted from Freud, this passage from Klein remains an assertion rather than an insight that is incorporated into her theory of child development, and nowhere does she spell out the way in which siblings can "provide the basis of a heterosexual position". It is clear from both Freud and Klein that they thought of siblings and nephews as important companions, but it is also clear that the effect of sibling attachment on psychic development has been difficult to incorporate into the main body of their thinking.

I do not share Klein's view that early sexual relations between brother and sister can provide a basis for a heterosexual position. Sexual relationships between brothers and sisters, at whatever age, as opposed to childish games of nurses and doctors, are likely to be a pathological resolution of parental neglect and a flight from oedipal conflict (Glenn, 1966; Bank & Kahn, 1982; Fleisher, 1990) rather than a helpful and creative solution. A. S. Byatt's novel *Angels and Insects* (1992) clearly illustrates the powerful and damaging effect that such a relationship can have upon adult sexuality. Yet I would want to agree with Klein that an affectionate and supportive relationship between siblings can ease the pain of oedipal conflict and can positively influence later relationships and the capacity to love.

I am going to use two clinical case histories to illustrate my view that sibling attachments can have a powerful effect upon the capacities to form adult relationships. In the first case there was a negative sibling attachment. In the second case there was a strong positive attachment.

Mrs K—Sibling rivalry: a negative sibling attachment

Mrs K was an attractive American woman in her early twenties, who came to see me because of her difficulty in working with women. She felt that women were always trying to manipulate her and outwit her, and that she was continually being forced to retaliate. From the moment that we first met, Mrs K cast me into the role of one of these cruel and punishing women. She saw me as someone waiting to laugh at her and ridicule her. Typically she would start a session with, "I woke up this morning. My heart was racing. I suppose you would say I was frightened. Right?" There would be a pause, filled with extreme pressure. If I confirmed her fear that she was frightened and that she had got it "right" her anxiety was not relieved. However, if I did not confirm her fear, she remained just as anxious. Which ever way I turned she saw me as cruel and punishing. She felt just as trapped by me if I began an interpretation with "I may have got it wrong but it occurs to me..." She could not hear what I wanted to convey, she could only respond to the word "wrong". She believed that I could not tolerate being "wrong" and so whatever I said she had to say I was right. The therapy continued in this dead stalemate for quite a long time. She would tell me something and then add "I know what you are going to say." What she meant was that she was saying something which she thought that I thought, and therefore she was hoping she was getting it "right". She seemed to be making an empty offering to an unappeasable God-like object. Who was this God?

I thought that what I should be looking for, in order to understand my patient's vicious superego, was a cruel introjected maternal figure, whose power may have been reinforced by a weak paternal presence (Glasser, 1985). Mrs K often let me know that she felt her mother saw her as a doll. It became clear that Mrs K had little expectation of being loved or accepted for herself, and I could see the part her mother's narcissism had had in Mrs K's intolerance of imperfection, her own or mine. Nevertheless there was something more to the impasse we experienced. My attempts to move into an area where Mrs K might find some relief met with a quite particular resistance. Nothing seemed to make a difference. She could only hear me as wishing to mock her or humiliate her.

I wondered whether her cruel superego was related to her father.

The adjective which she associated with men was "feeble". I also had had the experience of being seen as "feeble". This would happen when I would try to support her hard work and effort in therapy by commenting on the way in which she always arrived on time and never missed a session even when feeling ill. This offered her no relief. She said she felt me to be out of touch with her—which indeed I was. She felt I was making a comment from "afar", rather like her father's letters to her when he was away. Her "feeble" father had not been around enough in her childhood and her cruel superego did not seem to be linked to him.

I knew that Mrs K had an older sister but it had not occurred to me that the punishing figure which I was seen to be might be linked to her. (Perhaps because I had been an elder sister!) One day she brought a fragment of a dream in which she was going to the hairdresser. Her only association was that she had met her sister the day before. For the first time I wondered whether Mrs K saw me as her sister, and as soon as I began to wonder about this possibility with Mrs K, the transference began to unlock. Mrs K's sister was 12 years older than herself and there had been no other siblings. It became clear that Mrs K had been a much-hated younger sister who had displaced the older child from the favourite position. The older sister's natural jealousy seemed to have been compounded by the fact that she had been expected to act as "mother" to this hated usurper. Mrs K's father was fighting in Vietnam during her early years, and her mother was a librarian in full-time work. The older sister had been left alone with Mrs K, bringing her back from school and looking after her until their mother returned from work. This sister had been able to express her jealousy and rage in continuous mocking humiliation which was unmoderated by maternal concern. I came to believe that Mrs K had internalized this mocking humiliation as the predominant characteristic of relationships with older women and that this was the central fantasy she held about me.

I discovered with Mrs K that her experience with her sister had clouded her view of need and dependency and had distorted her original experience with her mother. It was this early dependency on her sister, as a quasi-parental figure, that complicated and confused the interaction between us. It was only when I became able to address the cruelty of her self-treatment directly in terms of her sister that I made any sense to her. Disentangling this transference opened the way later in the therapy to confronting the damage done by the actual maternal neglect. Meanwhile the central feature of our work became focused on trying to modify the stranglehold this internalized sister had upon Mrs K's way of relating to the world. It was quite striking that, once we began to work with this transference, Mrs K could begin to risk making a mistake, and at the same time she could allow herself to imagine that I could bear to be wrong. She began to give up her defensive strategy of trying to be perfect as she began to feel more able to deal with her fear that I might humiliate her. We could understand why she never missed a session and was always immaculately turned out. In time we could make sense of her earlier feelings that I had not understood her when I had supported her hard work. Her father had been away at war during Mrs K's early years and when he returned home on leave the family dynamics changed. Everyone appeared to be managing "perfectly". Mrs K had been left bewildered, enraged, and deeply disappointed that he could not understand her experience when he was not there. This was the transference experience that was re-enacted when I had supported her. I was felt to be out of touch with all the difficulty which was really going on for Mrs K.

Gradually Mrs K was able to move into a three-dimensional world in which she could imagine her sister to be a normal human being with strengths and weaknesses like anyone else. We discovered that secretly Mrs K felt inordinate guilt towards her sister, and this added to the difficulty of our work. She had always known that she was her mother's favourite child, and in spite of the real pain and suffering which she had experienced at her sister's hands there was a secret triumph. She knew that she had usurped her sister. Once Mrs K could acknowledge this belief she was able to imagine her sister's cruelty having its origin in jealousy and suffering. This realization allowed her to be able to make links to the women with whom she had difficulty at work. She inched towards becoming more compassionate both to herself and to others, not least myself. She came to see that neither I nor her colleagues were waiting to outwit her. She began to tolerate the times when I failed to understand her and was no longer overwhelmed by anxiety that I was inadequate. Her destructive rage and her wish to get rid of me, and the women at work, abated.

I am sure that the defence of perfectibility which Mrs K had developed in response to her sister's mocking humiliation had been reinforced by her mother's narcissistic investment in her. She believed she was her mother's favourite. But this favouritism was precarious and dependent upon being her mother's perfect little girl. She could not risk being noisy or dirty or rebellious. Mrs K had been trapped between wanting to be perfect, so as to outwit her sister, and wanting to be perfect, so as to keep her mother attached to her. The only way in which she could contain her despairing and murderous rage was to lash herself to the mast of her towering superego. Once we had both grasped the power that her sister held in her internal world, we began to be able to work more cooperatively and her punishing superego began to lose some of its force. This work then allowed us to return later to her earlier parental attachments.

Mr Y—Sibling love: a positive sibling attachment

Mr Y's relationship with his sister was as powerfully intense as Mrs K's relationship, but in a pleasurable and loving way. Mr Y was a young man who came to see me because, like Mrs K, he had found himself repeating an angry relationship with an older woman at work. He felt used and trapped by her. He also thought that she was behaving unprofessionally and wondered whether she was wishing to seduce him. Mr Y was the eldest of four children who were brought up by a succession of nannies and au pair girls. Within weeks of starting therapy Mr Y fell passionately in love with a girl who was younger than himself and he no longer felt trapped by the older woman at work. I was not sure how to understand this sudden eruption of feeling. I wondered if this affair was a flight from the therapy or if something had become unblocked. My strongest feeling was relief, for he seemed much happier and less angry with me. He began to miss sessions as he took his girl friend away for long week-ends, and I wondered with him whether he might see me as he had the older woman at work from whom he had to get away. This early period of work was turbulent and confusing and I was not sure what was happening. During this period I made a mistake in the monthly bill and charged him for an extra session. Mr Y reacted to my mistake with outrage which was followed by a sort of melancholic resignation. He said I had merely confirmed his belief that it was not safe to trust someone who was older, more knowing and mature than himself. I felt angry and indignant at such an exaggerated response, but I came to realize that I had been caught up in an unconscious enactment, though its exact nature I took quite a long time to understand.

In our first meeting Mr Y had been very angry when he spoke of his difficulties with the older seductive woman at work. I had imagined that these difficulties stemmed from a seductive but perhaps inconstant mother and that the role I was to play was of the older woman whose boundaries were not firmly held. When he almost immediately fell in love with a young girl I did not realize, in my feeling of relief, that I was responding to a split in the transference. Nor did I realize that the young girl into whose arms he had fled, from angry and frightening fantasies of older women, was his younger sister. Freud (1916) had said that "A human being's first choice of an object is regularly an incestuous one, aimed, in the case of the male, at his mother and sister" (p. 335). I learned, through working with Mr Y, that taking a sister as your first object choice is very different from taking your mother; at the very least the possibility of acting out the incestuous fantasy with a sister is more likely, as suggested by Melanie Klein (1975), and therefore the consequence of the choice is going to have a different effect. For instance, for I time I wondered whether Mr Y's love affair was a recovery of appropriate libidinal development. It was not until I overcharged him that I realized I had turned a blind eye to something that was going on between us. It had not occurred to me that he might be deeply attached to his sister, and that he was fleeing from a negative maternal transference into the arms of his sister.

I discovered that Mr Y and his sister had become very close at the time of the birth of two more siblings. They began to go off together. He was five and she was three and they created an imaginary world of their own. The nannies and au pair girls were only too pleased to look after two children who amused themselves all day. The world they created became increasingly fortified against the disappointments of the everyday world. Their father, a surveyor of oil rigs, was away for long stretches of time and their mother was a doctor who worked unmanageably long hours. The jealousy for their younger siblings was denied as they created a magic world for themselves. I often thought of the fairy tale of Hansel and Gretel when he told me of these years with his sister.

The therapy felt more contained once I realized that an aspect of Mr Y's love affair was a repetition of his flight from more difficult feelings of rage and melancholic despair. We were able to understand that his relationship with his sister had been of enormous comfort to him. It had protected him from the feelings I unconsciously evoked in him when I over-charged him. My unmindfulness linked back to his sense of a mother who withdrew in the face of the magic world he had created with his sister. He felt that I understood the relationship he had had with his sister, and our relationship became easier and more playful. I soon fell into another enactment. Mr Y was very sensitive and well-tuned to women when he liked them. He began to listen to everything I said with great imaginative understanding. I found myself looking forward to his sessions. Freud (1916–1917) believed that the oldest son is his mother's "undisputed darling". I felt Mr Y had become mine. I was not sure how this had come about. Why did I find him special? What was the nature of the fine-tuning we shared? When I was able to think that my experience of Mr Y might reflect the magic world he had had with his sister, I was able to understand that I had become his sister in the transference. I was able to see that, amongst the many things that this relationship had given him, it had created an experience of specialness. We were now in a position to understand the split in the transference which had happened at the very beginning. He realized he had fled from frightening fantasies of me into the magic world of his love affair as a defensive strategy for coping with the disappointments of absent parents, the jealousies of other siblings, and the comings and goings of nannies and au pair girls and therapist. We also came to see that his attachment to his sister had been of great benefit to him. It had helped him deal with the loss of a mother who was preoccupied with other babies and other people.

I hope that this account of my counter-transference struggle with Mr Y makes clear the important place held by his sister in his internal world. My experience with Mr Y when I was caught up in a sibling transference gave me the sense that this relationship had had many benefits. It had served in his mind as a model of how to love and cooperate; he knew about mutual dependence and he did not feel weakened and ashamed at it. I have not gone into the subsequent work which we went back to, namely his presenting problem with older women. There were unresolved oedipal difficulties which his relationship with his sister had helped him to avoid. But nevertheless I came to believe that his relationship with his sister had helped him in his relationships with women and, as Melanie Klein (1975) has suggested "developed . . . (his) capacity for love" (p. 223).

I began this paper with questions about why sibling relationships have been neglected in the psychoanalytic literature. In my view there may be a wish in us all to keep the children out, or up "the apple tree". In our failure to recognize a sibling transference, or to consider that it might be important, we may be treating siblings as though they are hated rivals for the theoretical space of parental relationships and transferences. We miss something important about the nature of sibling relationships if we only look at them as inhabiting the internal world as "second editions" of parents. I discovered that sibling attachments have a passionate intensity of their own, and when they appear in the transference they have a powerful effect on the therapy. I found myself much more vulnerable to a counter-transference enactment when the sibling transference was predominant. I came to realize that sibling attachments are not given up in the same way as parental attachments and that this brings a different dynamic to the sibling transference; it can feel more fixed or intransigent. I also found there was a reluctance to see myself as a much loved or much hated sibling. I felt safer and more in control in a parental transference. The two clinical examples I have given suggest that intense sibling attachments seem to be predicated upon parental absences. However, to then say that sibling attachments are merely parental substitutes is to miss the fact that the actual lived experience with siblings has its own consequences upon emotional development.

When Freud claimed that the passionate relationship that he had had with his nephew John determined all his future relationships with his contemporaries he was pointing to the important attachments which children make with one another. To suggest that this early way of relating had become "ineradicably fixed" in his psyche is to make the substantial claim that sibling attachments are never forgotten and have a lasting effect. I believe that Freud was right, and yet the place that these powerful attachments have been given in the theory of the inner world has been neglected.

Notes

1. The title of this paper is taken from the last five lines from T. S. Eliot's *Little Gidding*.
2. An earlier version of this paper was published in the *Australian Journal of Psychotherapy*, 1998, Vol. 17, Nos 1 & 2.

CHAPTER THREE

"I won't stand next to you when you throw bombs": addressing the perverse in the patient

Lorraine Colledge

Introduction

Working with highly perverse patients without corrupting the therapy is a frequent challenge for psychotherapists. There is an ongoing dilemma of needing to bring the perversity into the consulting room so that it can be known and understood, while simultaneously protecting the therapeutic process from becoming perverted. This paper describes work with a patient who had developed highly perverse internal structures and mechanisms as a way of surviving physical and sexual abuse, and details the ensuing developments and challenges in the transference relationship. It explores the initial use of the therapist as a good object who could bear to hear the horrors which had been survived, and then details the ways in which the perversity became more overt within the consulting room. The therapist was cast as helpless victim in the face of a perverse onslaught, and entreated to join a perverse partnership. The paper posits the existence of a "pseudo-victim" false self that was central in the maintenance of the internal perverse structures. The central interest lies in turning the patient's attempts to pervert the work into an advantage for the therapeutic process.

Introducing the patient

Jane was a white woman in her mid-twenties who was in therapy three times a week. She looked vulnerable and several years younger than her age, habitually wore trousers, and did not take off her coat during sessions. She said that she felt vulnerable when she had to wear fewer clothes during the summer. She did not use the couch, and continued to sit opposite me.

Jane entered the therapeutic relationship with unusual haste, and from the outset the therapy was characterized by a deluge of material which sustained itself for 3 years. Within 4 weeks, she had disclosed that inappropriate "sexual things" had happened within her family, and that later she had been sexually abused by a psychotherapist. It soon became apparent that she had survived prolonged physical and sexual abuse. In relating these experiences, Jane invariably appeared impassive, her face mask-like; she rarely moved in her chair.

Learning to see beyond the victim—identifying the patient's own perversity

Throughout the first year of therapy, a prolonged idealized transference appeared to offer Jane a position of safety from which she could talk about experiences of abuse. Her focus on the therapy was attenuated because, excepting her sessions, Jane lived an isolated life, the result of a combination of voluntary unemployment and a limited number of friendships. Increasingly the idealization appeared to be a narcissistic identification as she claimed that we shared the same thoughts, that "You and I are the same". The negative transference only seemed to be present through her fear of another abusing therapist: she had sudden images of kicking me when I moved slightly or changed position in the chair. At this point, she would believe that I was going to attack her, and this would be followed by her wish to kick out at me. Unsurprisingly, Jane could not use the couch and would become terrified if I appeared to be suggesting that she might do so.

At this time the challenges in the counter-transference appeared to be those facing any therapist when working with a survivor of abuse. I had to find ways of interpreting without being an abusive and intrusive penis–therapist. Jane was also concerned that I would become sexually excited by her material; on many occasions, I had to accept not knowing specific details because any attempt at clarification was experienced as excited curiosity.

In addition to the outpouring of family abuse, Jane's prolific presentation of dream material was a characteristic of this time. She brought violent and disturbed dreams to many of the sessions, often reading them out from a notebook. Initially, the recording seemed to enable her to contain the distressing material until her next session. Later, Jane's primary aim in reading out the dreams appeared to have changed. Her structured and pre-planned approach meant that she was able to minimize free association and to control her use of the session.

The volume and nature of the material made it difficult to work with her dreams, particularly in the early stages of the therapy. Sometimes it would take Jane 25 minutes to read out a dream without any associations or pause for thought. At other times, several dreams were brought to a single session. Thus I found it impossible to consider the material as it was being related without missing the next minutes of the dream; even remembering most of the content was a challenge. There were rarely any direct associations to the material, and although the dreams were often full of terror, they were initially related without affect. I started to become aware of a sly smile that would sometimes fleetingly pass across her face as she started to relate another atrocity.

The sly smile was my first intimation that Jane was not merely a survivor of abuse, and increasingly I started to wonder about Jane's motivations in bringing the material in this way. It seemed as though Jane was needing to evacuate the dreams, and to use myself and the therapeutic space as a repository for the disturbing images —while ensuring that it was not possible to work them through.

Many of Jane's dreams depicted family rows where repetitious arguments would end in violence, usually towards Jane but on occasions perpetuated by her. In dreams about her family, there was often confusion between sex and violence, and about appropriate relationships. Other dreams contained more bizarre images where good objects suddenly would become bad with beautiful birds turning into monsters or fireworks suddenly raining down on a party and burning people to death. There was often a persecutory and trapped quality with Jane locked in a house or prison, unable to escape the horrors because of patrolling wolves or sadistic guards. Most of the dreams were dominated by paranoid–schizoid processes.

A relentless quality was experienced in the counter-transference, as the bombardment of violent and disturbing dream images continued unabated, and as stories were related of sustained and extensive acting-out. Jane had previously engaged in petty theft from employers, in periods of uncontrollable promiscuity, and in drug and alcohol abuse. In the present, a sado–masochistic relationship was being acted out with an alcoholic boyfriend.

Initially, Jane only presented the damage that her boyfriend did to her—causing injury to her body, feelings and self-esteem. The physical damage was hidden as he never hit her face. However, it became increasingly apparent that while she did placate him in order to avoid violence, Jane would frequently taunt him. They had developed a well-worn pattern of intense argument usually relating to jealousy, occasional violence, desertion and reunion, and sex that included humiliation for Jane. There appeared to be an addictive bond that operated at a perverse rather than supportive level, and it appeared that moments of warmth and concern between the two were exceedingly rare.

When Jane told these tales, her sly smile would appear fleetingly. It seemed to me that when engaged in these activities, she would lose the capacity to think and only feel the addictive excitement and great rushes of adrenalin. She would then experience shock and terror when at real risk of bodily harm, but these more appropriate feelings would soon be lost again.

I often felt battered by the stories, and I struggled to encourage Jane to think actively about these experiences rather than endlessly recount them. It seemed that the interminable recounting in the therapy reflected the repetitious and sterile qualities of the relationship with her boyfriend. Initial movements in Jane were made by my making links with previous abuse and interpreting around her need for protection; this increasingly included acknowledgement that Jane needed protection from herself.

Jane's resentment at the inadequate protection she had received in childhood, and her sadism, were experienced in the transference. A session where further understanding was reached was sometimes followed by Jane immediately going to see her boyfriend for a further violent row. I became the helpless onlooker who was sadistically flooded with violent material and who held all of the concern. Initially I understood this in terms of Anna Freud's (1936) "identification with the aggressor". Jane was communicating to me the helplessness of the victim, while maintaining a more comfortable position for herself as the aggressor. With hindsight, reliance on this single theory was simplistic, and prevented me from identifying the core perversity sooner.

This became explicit during a series of incidents in the eighth month of therapy that highlighted the progress made, and Jane's underlying perversity. During a violent row with her boyfriend, Jane had been punched and kicked in the stomach; she felt that he might kill her. She managed to escape to the kitchen where she picked up a knife with the intention of killing him. Fortunately, she was able to "come to her senses" and start thinking. She put the knife down, and telephoned the police. The police duly arrived, and the boyfriend was arrested and charged. Jane was adamant that "he needed to be punished".

Her ability to start thinking, and to call for help indicated progress. However, she then engaged in some bizarre acting out. The formal action taken included a court injunction against the boyfriend going near Jane until the trial. However, within a few days it became intolerably exciting, and the forbidden couple began to meet for sex "behind the police's back". After an interpretation in the transference, Jane ashamedly admitted that one of the most exciting aspects for her was doing it behind my back as well. In this repetition compulsion, it seemed that the police and myself were representing the parents in her teens whom she precariously evaded and triumphed over while having a sexual relationship with her uncle. Possibly the perversion of "parental" concern was a retaliation for the inadequate protection she had received earlier in her life. However, it seemed to be the ultimate union in a sado–masochistic alliance where destructive forces dominated, and where good objects were triumphed over and made impotent.

The emergence of the sadistic abuser

As the therapy progressed in the second year, it became increasingly possible to identify and articulate Jane's active participation in these perverse happenings. She managed to leave her boyfriend whom she had frequently described as a monster. As her extensive acting-out and projection diminished, Jane had several dreams where monstrous growths would appear on her face, having come from inside her body. She became frightened about what was inside her; the "corruptness" that she had always felt was there seemed to be coming out. Now Jane was more often the perpetrator than the victim of violence in her dreams, it started to become apparent that Jane's own violence went beyond revenge and had an additional sadistic and perverse quality. However, the responsibility for this was often projected onto others with Jane determinedly maintaining a position of innocence, feeling righteous in her murderous actions. This "pseudo-victim" was pre-occupied with sadism and murderousness, disguised as the need for justice.

As Jane's aggressive and perverse aspects emerged more clearly, her ambivalence towards internal change increased. In a dream she "tended a sick man. She gave him something to drink to make him better—aware that he would think that it was poison. She then became preoccupied with whether it was poison or cure". Jane's wish to poison the therapy has often seemed stronger than her wish for cure, and she now often suspected my motives in seeming to help her. Her most frequent fantasy was that I was "in it for the money".

Throughout her second year of therapy, Jane wrote a novel about a young woman who had survived an abusive family. Drawing strongly on autobiographical details, the novel appeared to be informed by a paranoid–schizoid perspective, and enabled Jane to maintain a position as supreme victim while righteously acting out her vengeful and murderous fantasies on paper. In the part where she "takes her revenge", she is walking down a street, dressed in combat gear, holding a submachine gun. She then starts firing and mows down two policemen and her ex-therapist who are trying to stop her. It seems pivotal that she annihilates the parental figures when they try and stop her gross brutality, and not at the point when they fail to protect her. Jane became obsessed with the novel being published to great acclaim so that "the world would know how much I suffered". It became apparent that the "pseudo-victim" had a preoccupation with fame and universal recognition;

while the real victim often seemed to be terrified of discovery and to fear annihilation.

In the thirteenth month of therapy, Jane joined in the protestors in a dispute about the building of a major bypass.

> She had been there a while—everyone sitting around. She was watching from a distance. Seeing the police on their horses with their truncheons. Some were good-looking. She felt sexually excited by them. Clearly people were wanting a peaceful demonstration without violence; she realized that this was not what she wanted. She wanted the violence to happen. It was exciting when she looked at them.

Jane was sounding more and more excited as she told me; it was also in her expression, around her mouth and eyes.

> She joined a group of young people who were shouting at the police and throwing things. She started to do the same; she shouted at them; she could shout anything she liked. Then she was throwing things as well; anything she could find around. They backed the police down, and then the police would advance on them.

> She described this "dance" backwards and forwards several times; the police advancing with their truncheons, and then the group advancing with their missiles.

> She felt frightened when the police advanced on them and they were running away—she thought that everyone felt frightened. But then she felt very powerful when they advanced on the police; eventually surrounding one and throwing things at him.

This part was chilling to hear, and sounded murderous.

> She said that she thought she could do anything at that point. She ranted to me about fascists and abusers of power; these others in the group were allies and comrades that she shared thinking with. She felt sexually excited, but then thought to herself "No, you always avoid anger by doing that". By now they were in a nearby town, and she was hating the people watching them from the pavements. Hypocrites. Hating the things in the shop windows—hypocritical things—she wanted to smash them too.

When she finally stopped, I felt at a loss to know where to begin.
I decided to focus on the aspect that appeared most different:

LC: It seemed important to you that you had been fighting with
people—as part of a group.

J: Yes—I'm usually alone. It was very powerful together. We
shared ideals and beliefs. We could have done anything.
(another discourse about fascism and then continuing about
her family in a similar style of rehearsed litany). This time I
fought back and felt like myself.

LC: I wonder if there might be a way in which you felt like yourself
and very powerful because you were fighting back; but at the
same time, perhaps you hadn't felt in control, as though it all
had a force of its own.

J: Yes. Yes. I wanted it to go on forever and not stop. (Suddenly
her voice slowed and became despondent.) But I went into a
café to get some food. When I came out, the people had all
gone, and only the police were left. I felt so upset and
disappointed. I could have done anything before ... I felt
frightened to go into the house when I got home. How can I
feel so strong and then so weak?

LC: It seems that there are two different images of you around
today. One of feeling so powerful that it is as though you can
do anything and not be hurt—and one of weakness and
impotence.

The session finished shortly afterwards. The extent of Jane's non-
thinking state, and its dangers to herself and others was apparent. It
was also an indication of how therapeutic understanding was
subject to perversion. She "understood" that her violence and
hatred often became perverted into sexual excitement; during the
riot, her thought that "You always avoid anger by doing that"
became justification for violence.

During the riot, the omnipotent and murderous aspects of Jane,
alternating with the terrified and vulnerable ones, were illustrated
with new clarity. The confusion between sex and violence was again
present, as was the tendency to idealize in order to find allies that
had been evident in the transference. There was pathos in Jane
finding herself alone outside the café; the idealized alliances were
fragile and illusory.

The addictive excitement, and the omnipotent belief of being beyond harm, made acting-out difficult for Jane to give up. It gradually reduced although it was difficult for her to countenance having an "ordinary, boring life". Progress could only be made by continuous work on putting things into words rather than actions, facilitating her capacity to think, and by work in the transference.

Perverse partnerships and the transference

The work next moved into addressing Jane's own violent and perverse characteristics. It became apparent that we had been in a "honeymoon" period. Jane compulsively attempted to engage me as a perverse partner in a sado–masochistic battle. While Jane had the capacity for thought and reflection, there were times when she was dominated by her aggressive and perverse aspects while relentlessly talking about herself as a victim. At these times, her narcissism was extreme, and she would aggressively demand that I had to be "100% on her side". It was as though a perverse Jane was masquerading as a victim while neglecting the true vulnerable and needy aspects of herself. Here the pressure experienced in the counter-transference was to collude with the "pseudo-victim" Jane, who did not feel responsible for her actions. I had to learn quickly to differentiate between this pseudo-victim and the real survivor-victim who desperately needed help.

Counter-transferential feelings became critical in identifying the times when Jane was potentially actively murderous or aggressive, rather than simply feeling that way. If my counter-transference concurred with my observations, then I would make direct interpretation rather than interpreting at the level of her feelings. For example, it had previously been sufficient to talk about how much Jane might want to kick me, in order to contain her aggression. Then in one session, as her booted foot twitched while she talked of wanting to kick me, I felt unsafe. On that occasion, I told her firmly that she was not going to kick me because that was not acceptable, but that she could talk about feeling that way.

In another session, she appeared increasingly disturbed and schizoid as she talked again of murdering her abusers and herself. I often felt that Jane was capable of murder in this state of mind, and that she wanted me to condone this course of action. She reiterated that I had to be on her side in this.

LC: Well, I am on your side—on the side of the part of you that wants to be healthy.

J: (Paused) Yes. (then stridently). The most loyalty, the ultimate loyalty, I have known was last year when I wrote to my friend saying that I wanted to put a bomb under the House of Commons. And would she be next to me if I did. And she wrote back saying that she would be right next to me.
(J was moved to tears at this "loyalty"—I felt shocked that she had found another perverse partner)

LC: And I won't stand next to you when you throw bombs. Or when you put them under yourself or your therapy. Or when you put yourself at risk. I'm on the side of your becoming more healthy, and feeling better.
(J nodded and seemed to relax).

It seemed critical to use such opportunities to articulate my commitment to working towards Jane's health, and to align myself with the part of her that wished to be healthy. This had to be repeated on several occasions as she was not able to hold it in mind. Jane appeared to experience relief when I refused to become a perverse partner, but seemed compelled to keep trying to engage me in this way.

On another occasion, she spent the last session before a long break talking about suicide. This was not unusual, but now there was an added motif of a death skull that she kept seeing. As I went to close the session, feeling worried about leaving her in this state, Jane sneered at me "I can see the death skull again". Her noxious sadism infuriated me, and I became aware that any feeling of concern was diminishing.

There were times when I felt untouched by her attempts, and was able to carry on thinking. At other times, on leaving a session, I would experience either a wish to admit defeat, or such anger and outrage at the constant bombardment that I wished very much to retaliate and put my own bomb under the therapy. I started to wonder again about the problems with her parents in her teens; in my frustration, the rows with her father which ended in violence, and the threat of the "school for bad girls" were increasingly seeming understandable.

Holding the perversity in the transference often felt fragile yet Jane was having occasional sessions where she was able to think and reflect about her murderously perverse aspects, so I felt that some assimilation of my interpretations was happening. In one session, she had been able to think and talk about the destructive parts of herself. It ended positively, with a sense of containment and further understanding. However, the following session was very chilling as she recounted leaving the positive session:

J: When I left here, I felt really good. Much more in touch. I walked down the street, and my mind felt really positive and powerful ... Then I thought ... about how I could release ... all the murderous thoughts.
(Her voice kept faltering towards the end as she lost words—there was a long pause before continuing in a manic tone.)
The best way I can describe it, although it sounds weird, was that I could have a "feast of murder".
(She excitedly elaborated a fantasy about "butchering" everyone as she walked, repeating that it would be a "feast of murder".)
There was blood and gore everywhere. I felt very excited.

LC: (I felt cold. I decided that I had to be direct and quick). I think that something happened when you left here. You had been able to look at the very destructive parts of yourself with me, and perhaps having help to do that had made you feel good. But when you left, while walking down the hill, the murderous and destructive side took over again. You and I had not been in support of you being murderous—but somehow things got twisted round so that it felt as though feeling murderous was positive.

J: (became tearful) Yes.

LC: And I think that you just went back into that state of mind now when you talked about what happened on the hill, and that you have just left it again.

J: Yes—it seems to come and go very quickly. It's very disturbing.

This illustrates how quickly Jane moves between states of mind. It resonates with Steiner's (1992) description of how the movement between paranoid–schizoid and depressive positions "can be seen in the fine grain of a session, as moment to moment changes". Jane's rage when she feels abandoned at the end of a session was indicated, and also her perversion of analytic understanding.

An aspect that had not been apparent to me at the time emerged in the following weeks. It became increasingly clear that the perverse parts of Jane found it unbearable when they were understood and known by me. These parts then turned on the analytic understanding and perverted it, while also wishing to destroy me. Although there were undoubtedly envious components in the attacks, they seemed to be more motivated by a rage in "being known". On another occasion after being understood in her destructiveness, Jane had a fantasy after the session of "plunging her hands into a woman's stomach and ripping out her organs".

It was as though the needy parts of Jane were desperate for help, while the destructive parts could not bear to be known and understood. It has been an ongoing challenge to try and maintain a working alliance with the needy Jane, while not mistaking the pseudo-victim for the needy Jane. Identifying the authentic experience in the consulting room has been crucial. At the end of the session that included the "feast of murder", Jane said that she thought that part of her was very arrogant. She looked down shamefaced, but then looked up with a fleeting triumphant glance. She said "Just now, when you said about us working together against the destructive part of me—I—I don't mean to sound rude—but I wanted to laugh at you. There was this voice in my head that said "You'll never win". She sounded manic.

Here the opposition to progress by Jane's destructive aspects, and her wish to engage in a perverse battle is overt. It felt frightening to be with her on this occasion, although I had not feared physical violence—it was the exposure to such horror that often felt almost overwhelming.

While interpreting in the transference about her apparent wish to engage me in a perverse relationship was occasionally helpful, at other times it became very exciting for Jane. In a session during the twentieth month of therapy, I became aware that yet again Jane had seemed excited while bombarding me with violent, perverse images. I found myself wishing that I could stop seeing her. I decided to concentrate on the process.

LC: I understand that what you have been telling me is important
to you, but perhaps it would be helpful to think about what it
is like to say those things to me. I wonder if perhaps there
might be some pleasure for you in talking about the violent,
destructive parts of yourself to me—as though I just have to
listen passively.
(Jane smiled, and nodded in acknowledgement while I said
this.)

J: (With great excitement) You don't have to be passive! You can
be active! Be active!

LC: And perhaps join you in a sado–masochistic frenzy.

J: (laughs manically) Yes.
(Pauses. Collects herself.)
Well, I do have to express these things (she grinned sadistic-
ally) and you are my therapist.

LC: So it's as though I just have to sit here.
(Suddenly there was a grotesque smile that was like a
horizontal slash across her face. Her hand went up to cover it.)

J: I keep wanting to laugh. About sadism. Frenzy. It's not
deliberate.

It should be noted that when in a thinking state of mind, Jane
is very aware of her dilemmas, and psychologically articulate.
Sado–masochistic was a term that she had long used to describe
herself and her relationships. Here the entreaty to become a
perverse partner is explicit. The roles are specifically allocated: the
listening therapist placed in the masochistic position by the sadistic
patient.

I remain unsure as to the usefulness of my interpretation about
the sado–masochistic frenzy. It did prompt a greater articulation of
Jane's transference at this point, but it may also have added to the
intensity of her feelings. I have increasingly come to believe that,
when working with perversity, there is not a finite amount of
disturbed material that the therapist can seek to bring into the open.
Rather it would seem that patients with this level of perversity may
simply feed on "bad food" and use it to nourish the more corrupt
aspects. There is a therapeutic task to enable the patient to articulate
the full psychological dilemma while not adding to the seemingly
infinite reserves of perverse excitement.

Transference and an internal concentration camp

One of the challenges of this work has been to try and move quickly with Jane's states of mind—particularly when the shifts appeared to be from moment to moment. Towards the second year of therapy, a new constellation of imagery about concentration camps emerged. Jane felt by turns like a Nazi or a Jew in a schizoid alternation. She veered between sneering identifications with the Nazis which included crying over Hitler's death and having masturbatory fantasies about Nazis, to then being sickened at Nazi atrocities and crying in a deluded state for herself and "their other victims". At times, the shifts happened from moment to moment. It was counter-productive to interpret her vulnerability when she was in a Nazi state of mind—she would sneer back at me. If I interpreted her sadism too slowly, she would have shifted and it would be directed at the oppressed and vulnerable Jane who would then feel persecuted and misunderstood by the Nazi-therapist. The most valuable progress was made by seizing the moments when Jane was able to think. Then I interpreted how she might feel like both a Nazi-persecutor and an oppressed Jew, and that the concentration camp might be just how it felt inside her mind.

Wolf in sheep's clothing: the importance of pseudo victims

The use of a pseudo-victim false self by a patient appears to have multiple functions. I believe that it is primarily a mechanism by which the perverse self seeks to ensure its own survival: the patient is defended against the knowledge of his or her own sadism and perversity through the adoption of the pseudo-victim role. Suffering seems to be the central experience, and it is a suffering that the world should know about—it has almost messianic qualities. The patient also appears to experience the role of victim as providing permission for any type of behaviour. Thus Jane believed herself to be beyond reproach, and in her more disturbed times had been clear that murder would be a justifiable course of action for her. She appeared shocked when I did not appear to reinforce this. Thus Jane was able to maintain a position of omnipotence and omniscience as other people, including her therapist, could never have a full understanding of her suffering and pain. This appears to be a particular version of Rosenfeld's (1987) destructive narcissist who sees the self as the source of all goodness. The challenge for the therapist is in identifying who is in the consulting room at any given moment in order to avoid colluding with the pseudo-victim yet not failing to respond to the needy patient.

CHAPTER FOUR

Impasse and empathy[1]

Robert Royston

Introduction

This chapter proposes that there is a level at which analytical
meaning is boundaryless and universal, that there is no
problem about communication across cultural, gender,
lifestyle and political divides, and that in the analytical encounter,
if it is operating in a certain mode, chalk can understand cheese with
no serious obstruction or problem. It is argued that such
communication is achieved through a level of understanding that
passes through barriers, making contact with the seemingly un-
contactable, and that the mode is empathy. This will be illustrated
with reference to work with an abusive patient demonstrating the
working of this analytical mode, and it's capacity to transcend
difference.

Of course there are surface difficulties. In the consulting room
and elsewhere we are told or hear things that are strange to us.
What is bush medicine, or obeah? What is Kataze root? Why was a
child half blinded by a cricket ball treated with local applications of
mother's milk? Alien practices, alien cultures. An Italian–American
film director, interviewed on television told how as a boy in New

York he could have become a Mafioso. These were men who were special, respected, rich, connected with other awesomely special men. But the director didn't try to work for them and the fact he didn't, he says, means nothing in terms of difference between him and them. He happened to take a different fork in the road.

I, as a therapist, think about this story with scepticism. In my world a psychopathic tendency, a corrupt super ego, an infantile personality and unbounded sadism are a prerequisite to working for the Mafia. But the director has insisted this is not the case. A cultural difference, then, within a shared white middle-class intellectual world. Could I understand this difference in the consulting room or would the patient and I be at odds? A female patient, a lesbian and radical feminist, coming for an initial interview, hates me on sight. It's because I am a man. Can I understand this?

Understanding through granite, this is what I wish to explore. I'm not referring to the standard intellectual, insightful, intuitive, compassionate, verbal form of understanding that has been the staple of psychoanalysis for a century. I mean understanding on another level. I am proposing that there is a level at which understanding is boundaryless and universal, a way of being with a patient that undercuts cultural, gender, political and other differences. It is a mode that, in it's working, is close to dream. In fact, this position, developed from Thomas Ogden's (1994) formulation about "inter-subjectivity" is a quintessential psychoanalytical position.

It is not my intention to imply that psychotherapy is easy. We know it isn't. It is definitely difficult. However the difficulty is eased by something that is the opposite of difference. Both parties are on the same side, at least in the matter of analytical goals. We want the same thing. But here's the rub—do we really have similar goals: health and progress? First, our idea of what health is may differ. Suppose the patient likes being a practising sado–masochist and visiting fetish clubs. I think this practice is not psychologically healthy and a product of trauma, woven symbolically into a ritual. Address the underlying trauma, the childhood characterized by a mixture of deprivation and psychological abuse, and the perversion will lose its capacity to fascinate. The patient, on the other hand, hopes the analysis will make the perversion more exciting.

This poses a difference to be overcome; a fantastic challenge in the psychotherapy. It has to work in such a way that the patient comes to see that the perversion, exciting as it is, indeed helpful to him as it has been in some ways, isn't his friend. It's a seductive and powerful enemy. It stands in the way of progress, breakthrough, and an end to the cycle of pain and failure.

But there's another type of problem, which is more common and more difficult still, that is a powerful factor with a particular category of patient. With such people there is a good initial period, when the patient is supported and becomes more stable. Work progresses and insight is gained, then suddenly everything goes flat and nothing changes. Increasing understanding appears to bring increasing stasis. A horizontal split has occurred, that is a split between surface and depth. On top the patient works within the analytical mode and change is sought through insight, emotional release, and containment. But a far more potent and obdurate subterranean continent is soon glimpsed. This undersea world is the real area for analytical focus and struggle. And here the patient and the therapist are implacable foes, in terms of the very long-term goals that they had hoped were common. The therapy is treated as though inimical to the patient's well being. Health—as seen by the therapist—appears to be psychic death to the patient, so ardently does he resist the analysis, secretly, beneath the harmonious surface.

This is real difference. In this watery and distorted world, the therapist, who feels his interpretations to be helpful, is heard speaking the language of critical denigration. The patient feels he is doing nothing wrong yet the therapist feels frustrated and attacked. These dynamics suggest that the patient has hard-core character resistances, not the defensive resistances of the neurotic patient. These are obdurate and offer a menacing challenge to the effectiveness of therapy. Such patients are variously named in psychoanalysis, for example as "high level borderline patients" by Kernberg (1975)—that is patients whose borderline personality structure is rigid rather than labile and crypto-psychotic. They may be described as schizoid, as narcissistic, or autistic, or as demonstrating obsessional character disorder. Usually all of these phenomena are present to some degree, particularly narcissism, a condition Kernberg has described as virtually untreatable. The problem is a potentially chronic difference between therapist and patient, in which the patient blocks the cure and deletes the therapist from the analytical encounter, reducing her, the therapist,

to a very important shadow or a totally un-worrying ghost at the
great feast which is the patient's self. The case material that I will
introduce following the section on empathy will provide more
details about this sort of patient, helping to establish the nature and
extent of the problem and a way of working with it.

Empathy

I am proposing that it is through empathy that we are able to
understand and make contact with this type of patient, but this
sounds too weak and evokes criticism. Empathy is thought of as tap
water among therapists, counsellors and psychoanalysts. Besides,
empathy is not an analytical mode. We may need it, just as we need
compassion and a wish to help, but we tend to think of it as the
outer envelope rather than the piece of paper with the message.
Interpretation is the essential analytic mode. And interpretation
relies on a healthy degree of distance. It is hard edged. It works a bit
like this (to exaggerate): there's a problem, pin it to the drawing
board; there it is, out there.

Of course, we formulate our interpretations with an intuitive
mind and with sensitivity, and without "memory and desire", as
Bion (1970) recommended, but nevertheless with rationality, even
though this rationality is prompted into mysterious being by an
unconscious nudge. The therapist is still thinking. In the background we have our paradigm, developed through our reading, our
learning, our experience and orientation. What we see or intuit is, in
a sense, what we know.

Unless we have a theoretical model buried somewhere in our
minds we will not be able to recognize the tricky unconscious
phenomena in the patient's associations. Our insights seldom go
beyond our theoretical model, no matter that we listen carefully to
our patients, with open minds, rather than with heads bustling with
jargon and concepts.

Another objection to the idea of empathy that we need when
faced with these particular patients is that this is merely another
way of referring to counter-transference. The therapist uses her
personal responses as a cognitive instrument, analysing them in the
service of reaching a greater understanding of her patient. Bion

urged a deeper engagement still, encouraging us to forget memory and desire so that we might be able to approach each session anew, becoming wholly engaged in it. However, what I am proposing here is something rather different. It is a further development of analytical technique, a development of the use of counter-transference, though I think quite a dramatic one. Thus my argument is that there are seemingly intractable problems in the treatment of certain difficult patients. But there is a technique, or rather a mode of consciousness, or attention, which melts differences. This method is empathy, but of a very particular sort. Furthermore, it is my contention that this problem—the massive obdurate character resistances of a certain type of patient and the patient's seeming attack on the cure—has been theoretically misconceived by psychoanalysis because the concept, the mode, of empathy was not fully developed or accepted.

Analytical problems

Some of the most commonly encountered problems that emerge in long-term analysis with high level borderline patients involve the deletion from analysis of the therapist as a productive contributor, and the domination of the patient and his or her habitual psychic *modus vivendi*. With such patients the therapy can be a long struggle to keep analysis in place against very persistent attempts to import into the consulting room other modes, which don't come from the therapeutic field at all, such as coaching, tuning, management, amputation, injection, exhibiting, purgation, freezing and cleansing. Psychoanalytic psychotherapy has ardently sought methods of working with this radical difference between patient and therapist, because failure means clinical analysis is limited to patients who have a core of health, a functional ego.

The first problem encountered with high level borderline patients, is this: The therapist and his comments are subtly wiped out or demoted from higher order interpretative statements into the common or concrete, such as advice, instruction, psychological coaching, or something more crude. For example, I say to a patient, "You're afraid of applying for this job not so much because you fear failing, but because you fear success—I say this because you told me how you felt your mother withdrew from you after successes, and seemed much more accepting of you when you were ill, than when you were strong".

The patient appears to wrestle with this in a productive manner. He seems pleased with developments. The next session he has forgotten everything.

"Drat. What was it?" Then he begins to remember, "Oh yes, you said I was lazy and needed a kick in the arse—I agree".

This interchange illustrates two important factors, the reduction of the mind of the therapist to a faculty that is productive only of clichés and lower order functions, (psychotherapy is coercive) and also an omnipotent capacity to reorganize reality, to virtually invent my comment. The patient invented me in his own image, as crass and bullying. This is what Kohut (1971) calls the "alter ego transference" or "twin-ship transference". I interpreted. He couldn't understand.

What was I saying? Could I repeat please?

I repeated. He got it! Excellent. Ah, but now it was all going rather vague. Words were crumbling. Forgetting was taking place before our very eyes. "What had I said, what?" Could I repeat? Please repeat.

By the time he understood what I was saying I had had to simplify my comment. He then got it securely and kept it after it had been milled on a wheel of incomprehension. But now it was a cliché. Its modest insight and everything that characterized it as particular, contextual, had been squeezed out.

"My problem is I don't remember things", was how it came out.

This sort of patient's exploitive behaviour and the wiping out process has been seen by Kernberg (1975) and by Kleinians (Klein, 1957) as envious. The patient simply wants to be the be-all and end-all and self sufficient with the store of good things in the world locked up inside. These good things, which the therapist wants to contribute, cannot be experienced as coming from without. That engenders envy. So the wiping out and redefining process ensures that the patient's subjective experience is that all things good emanate from the self, and all things bad emanate from without. The envy is created by the fact that the patient is inwardly starved, empty, himself a cliché, say Kernberg and Klein, and is so precisely because the other person, the world with its source of nourishment, has been wiped out by the patient's constitutional aggressiveness and sadism. To see richness in others is intolerable, therefore. Let's then, look for a moment at another dynamic: another process by which the patient strips the other person of ownership of mental richness. This is the arrogation of the therapist's statement to the self.

I make a comment to the patient and she reacts warmly, quickly but on a tangential axis. I have said that she feels needy but is anxious as to whether the therapy is safe or whether, if she comes to rely on it, I will try, like her father, to control and dominate her thinking. She says, "Yes, very much so, it's about my confusion and excitement. I don't know what happens to me but maybe it's tension, but when I'm with other people I get a bit crazy and hyper. Why am I so tense do you think? It's this, like, exploding feeling in my head. Well, then I get drunk and I sort of get the strangest ideas popping into my head from nowhere—it's as though I haven't got a home in my head, any old stranger can stumble in. Why does that happen? I wish I knew why that happened."

By slow degrees and many digressions the patent worked her way through a variety of subjects, all of which posed a tangential question and then circled her way back to where we had started from, saying: "You know, what occurs to me is that perhaps I feel homeless as though I've left home to get away from my father. I'm getting the feeling this could be a big thing with me, not having a home, I think it affects the way I feel here."

The response is off the point, another subject is spoken of—confusion—a mention is made of her head as a home, but this doesn't really refer to the interpretation—through all of this my interpretation is put in a little capsule and sealed away, there's a time gap, and then the interpretation is reintroduced, but now as the patient's own insight phrased in a slightly modified form. The modification, as well as the delayed uptake, severs the connection between the contributor and the recipient, so that in the patient's subjective world she is the sole generator of good things, un-reliant on people outside, whom she may treat with coldness and contempt.

This patient feels particular antipathy towards the therapist when the latter is experienced as helpful and creative. This antipathy can be quite aggressive, but hidden, and actually often takes place outside the session, or just omnipotently in the patient's mind. It may take a concrete form, when, for example, the patient gets drunk after a good session. In a type of symbolic act, the session's curative potential is drowned or vomited up because it derives from other and not from self.

This process—of excretion without digestion—is typical of the type of borderline character–disturbed patient I am talking about here. And as you can see, it creates a wall of difference between the therapist and the patient. These and other narcissistic phenomena are seen in psychoanalysis as a major obstacle to therapeutic progress, particularly so as the patient appears to derive increased strength and stability from paralysing the therapeutic encounter: he then becomes dependent on this process, with the treatment secretly functioning not as analysis, but as a type of pathological support system, based on the patient's exercise of power.

Some patients can use therapy quite well but in a limited way just as long as the therapist does not refer to the transference. If the therapist says, for example, "In the dream I think you are the princess and I am the slave", she would get into trouble, for introducing herself into the equation. If she said, "What you have described happening in your work is like you and me here. I might, like the boss, be poised to throw you out", you feel she would be told this was pretentious rubbish, the patient knew all about it, it was the sort of thing you were supposed to say in this sort of therapy and it was meaningless, and also annoyed her a lot and she wished the therapist would just say to herself, I am just not going to do this any more.

Now transference is the heart of psychoanalysis. It distinguishes it from all other therapies. Of course what's also visible here is the proscription of another *sine qua non* of analysis, the unconscious. The transference is the unconscious writ large and dramatized. So the patient attacked the *modus vivendi* of psychoanalysis, its heartbeat, and replaced it with support and sympathy.

Can one glimpse something beneath this interchange? Psycho-analysis is a process of solving a mystery only to find another beneath it. It is repeatedly said that patients like this destroy the creativity and vitality in the therapist, and attack mental content and the whole process of thinking. But if we look more deeply we might see that the attacking patient may be responding to a damaging object. This again touches on the matter of differences, theoretical differences within psychoanalysis that may lead to a difference in how a patient is seen and treated.

I will now demonstrate the working of radical empathy, as described by Ogden (1994) and also by Kohut (1971), and show how it works like a metaphorical translator that facilitates comprehension creating an overarching bridge—or should that be a tunnel— along which meaning can flow.

Example one: the abusive patient

This is a man in his late twenties whose previous attempts at therapy had failed.

The patient from the start said that he felt I was strange. Certain practices appeared weird to him, such as that I didn't ask him how he was as I opened the door to him. I interpreted this as a failure in my provision. But this got nowhere, was swept aside. His attitude developed into more direct and less focused attacks. My plants were sickly; the neighbourhood was "sleazy". My room was said to be badly organized, lop sided, crazy. Then the patient became more explicitly attacking and would, in answer to an interpretation, roar, "fuck off". I was described in abusive terms. He threatened to make wide-ranging enquiries about me and made veiled hints that he might report me to some type of ethical watchdog, though the charges would be vague. During the first few months he would often minutely examine his fingernails and clean them, run his fingers through his hair and shake out dandruff, rub his eyes, groan, and cough loudly and graphically, finally spitting into a tissue. There was something riveting but profoundly offensive in all of this, particularly the rich and phlegmy coughs and the detailed throat-clearing hawks.

The patient's manner and style was rich in subtext. Therapy was a waste of time, an interruption of one's bathroom activities, or no different from those activities, a crude expulsion of mental detritus. There were other meanings, but his actions also involved the abusive exposure of a trapped person, the therapist, to what is usually, and courteously, veiled as private. Watching him repetitively cough and clean himself, one was an imprisoned witness to a private act. The invisible structure of civility—our respective identities, our set-piece relations—was torn down. Me therapist, you patient, we have important work to do: that paradigm was not on the radar screen of consciousness. There was no such template.

We were two people together in a room for no purpose, less connected than dice in a dice cup.

My first thoughts ran along obvious lines. He was projecting something chaotic and dirty in himself or in his experience into me and in the room. He was attacking and soiling the environment. He was an aggressive bully. He was making me experience something he had experienced—abusiveness, insult, intrusion, aggression, denigration. Some therapists I think would have said his behaviour was a destructive attack on the good breast or on the creativity of the analytical encounter. Kleinians (Klein, 1957) might see an attack on the parental couple in intercourse, while some therapists might have thought about termination, because the patient did not seem to want analysis or therapy.

But it wasn't always like this. Some sessions were fairly normal although the thread of contact was ceaselessly broken because he wiped everything out. Each good session was a one off. Nothing was built up. Sometimes he seemed to eagerly take up something I said, but in reality he was putting his own slant on the interpretation, stamping himself over it, supplanting it. Sometimes a good interpretation one day was next day repeated as rather menacing. This seemed further evidence that the patient was paranoid—it was really he who was menacing and venomous. I interpreted along these lines, and linked the comments with his attacks on me. This seemed to make sense. We seemed to be getting somewhere, but still no residue of agreed truth resulted. And the aggressive attacks continued unabated with the same contempt and ferocity.

Now all this is really the story about how I got it, or hit on the truth. There was impasse until comprehension came through the form of the empathy I have been trying to describe. During one particular session, I was listening with free floating attention, not thinking, lost in reverie of no particular shape or colour or theme. This wasn't the counter-transference. In the counter-transference I continued to feel insulted and professionally negated. But I pushed this aside and followed a trail of images that blew across my unfocused imagination. I tried to pick up significance in the minimal fluff and invisible detritus of the mind that listens absent-mindedly.

The idea here, a concept of Thomas Ogden's (1994), which he calls inter-subjectivity, is that patient and therapist communicate in an underground way to create a type of third presence. This is a phenomenon that includes the subjectivity of the therapist and of the patient. The therapist unconsciously weaves his own private material around that of the patient's, and the product is something like this.

I found myself picturing a circus with clowns and acrobats, and then a cavalcade of clowns and acrobats and troubadours going down a country road. Then monkeys playing in trees. Everything faded a bit and I remembered my children's playground and the monkey bars and children hanging upside down, and the ceaseless call of children to be looked at. All this was minor; in the corner of the eye, so to speak, I noticed the patterns of sunlight on the curtains. I thought about all of this for a moment and everything speeded up into a chain of connections. I remembered how my patient came from a milieu where complete openness and frankness, to the point of rudeness, was highly valued. I though of the classical analytical suggestion to the patient that they simply say whatever came to mind without censorship, and thought of the grinding difficulties I and my colleagues often have with highly defended resistant patients. All this in a moment. Then I made a connection to theoretical constructions, and to Kohut's (1971) description of the narcissistic transferences, particularly the alter ego or twin-ship transference, where the patient sees the therapist as the same as himself. And, of course, I got it in the proverbial blinding flash.

The patient's unrestrained behaviour, his entirely horrible behaviour, took on another meaning. Previously it could be seen as profoundly disrespectful and explicitly as well as cryptically abusive. That's how it felt in the counter-transference. But that was a counter-transference misunderstanding based on the disengagement of a deeper level of empathy, what we may call regressive empathy. So was my thought that he was attacking the analytical process a misconstruction? In fact the openness and uninhibited behaviour of this patient were forms of self-display. He was in a way giving himself to me, entertaining me. Of course, there were huge differences here in that I didn't find him in the least bit entertaining or amusing. Nevertheless my vestigial and peripheral fantasy revealed that he was the performer, clown, emotional acrobat, agile child. I was meant to be impressed. If insult was intended and often it was, the insult and its style were to be admired for its spontaneity. His cursing me was meant to be a sign that he valued and trusted me, that we were so close and mutually trusting that he could do what he liked. This was a sign of how wonderful the therapy was. How wonderful I was. Uninhibited self-exposure is valued in psychoanalysis as everyone knows. Shouting "fuck off" showed he was a rare patient, special, different, with a special therapist.

So to focus on the attack without due regard for the patient's sense of it as a gift is to insult the patient. And such patients are easily insulted because the analytical situation triggers a profound and urgent need in them for approval. In patients who have been starved of uncritical admiration in childhood, this need isn't only a hunger but a developmental necessity. To interpret along standard lines is to be seen as a critical rejecter of the patient's, or this patient's gift: the gift of the self in full agile display. The coughing and the insulting disregard for the niceties of the analytical project was a form of unveiled offering of the self. His soiling attack on me and on the environment were retaliatory, because he felt wounded and insulted by my comments which, with a different patient, would have been very ordinary and benign.

The standard analytical *modus vivendi* is based on attention to the transference neurosis: liberation through insight and through emotional release in the containing environment, the removal of repression and blocks to emotional discharge, liberation through linking destructive past with the state of the internal world in the present. This standard transference implies distance, and self-transcendence—that the patient can separate from the process and the self and reflect *post facto*. But this patient was a performing child who needed, for a time, to be held in the special envelope of attentive parental approval.

Understanding of this need led to big changes in the therapy and the patient. The abusive and hyper aggressive elements abated, then ceased. The patient did excellent work and startling growth ensued. How was this achieved? Through attention to what Ogden (1994) calls the analytical third—the jetsam of the therapist's mind—the therapist may pick up the thread of something like a dream, and which can be analysed just as a dream can. In a way, though, it is the patient's dream running around the edges of the therapist's mind, though the material it uses is emphatically your own.

I think this is an example of empathy or attunement melting differences. I referred earlier to seemingly intractable resistances in analysis, how the patient deletes the therapist from the encounter and arrogates everything to the self. This type of patient acts as though they feel that what the therapist offers is an attack on the self. Just as the patient above wanted to swing on the monkey bars and show off and be loved, so the borderline or narcissistic patient often feels that the therapist's interpretations are showing off. They feel diminished by the "brilliance", as they see it, of the therapist. Such patients are vulnerable to a subsidence of the self. They have to block out the other person because they feel asset-stripped by the liveliness of the other. It is as though two people cannot be potent or fecund in the same dialogue. Only one can. The other suffers. They want to be the one that is alive and creative, as they see it.

What is important about what I have been describing, is that it melts this difference because the patient (unconsciously) senses the interpretation as a mutual product. What one says is subtly different. It has a more inquiring tentative quality. It is quite a way from a picture of the patient and therapist as locked into disparate roles. It's the deepest possible form of mutuality in the psychoanalytical project. The interpretation is the product of both people together. In fact it can even feel that it is the product of neither. Though it applies to both. For these reasons it is not a demonstration of the superiority of the therapist.

Through this process I was able to find a level of warmth and liking for my patient that was only possible after I had grasped the nature of his abusive behaviour. I needed to understand that it was an attempt to impress, that his aggressive intrusiveness was a way of implanting in me an image of himself as prodigiously unforgettable. I interpreted this, being careful not to stigmatize it as destructive, but instead dwelt on his feelings of specialness, how he could feel excluded and undervalued and unnoticed.

Example two: the stuck patient

Here is another example.

A patient had been locked into what appeared to be a chronic resistance. His life was frustrating and difficult. He overworked and on top of this was a fitness fanatic, driving himself to train no matter how depleted he felt. His job was imperilled by his hard-line antagonistic, demanding attitude to his staff, and his tendency to despise the rules and standard way of doing things.

In the session he talked in his usual manner, detailing problems, but without any expression of pain or emotional difficulty. His talk ranged here and there, about conflicts with people at his health club and at work, about how people have cautioned him to approach matters more circumspectly. As I listened and allowed my thoughts to meander I vividly recalled a picture I had seen years previously. I had not thought about this for a decade. It was, I think, a photograph in a collection of American images, and showed a young boy in an alarmingly realistic stance pointing a toy gun at the back of a pedestrian. Behind him a tattered wall poster advertised a film, which as I recalled, was about a gunman on the run. The text was to do with how this outlaw was un-catchable. But there was one man only who might do it. There was a picture of the craggy faced law enforcer and another of the lawbreaker alone in a lonely alley. Did I simply imagine, or accurately remember, that the outlaw's face was lined with prison bars, as though he carried these with him everywhere like a contraption or a headpiece?

I said to the patient, with much trepidation as there was no evidence, that he might feel lonely, lost, hunted, deprived without support or appreciation, but while that was a painful situation it might also be heroic, maybe romantic: a lone hero doing things his way and shooting from the hip, demanding achievement from his staff, kind of as though he was an outlaw, un-captured, untamed.

To my relief this instantly rang a bell and the whole tone of the session changed and became more emotional. This insight might have been reached through another, more intellectual route by analysis of the patient's material, out there on a screen as it were but I believe that this entry point would have excited the patient's resistances. He would have sensed me as the lawman sent to capture him. By arriving at the suggestion a different way, this was avoided. It is as though the image of the urban sheriff was put into me by the patient. It was something we had almost created together drawn from my experience and from his.

Conclusion

Every psychoanalytic treatment must go through phases. The *modus vivendi* settles, then is disrupted and changes. Conflict and aggressive expression is inevitable and usually has a positive outcome. The mode of empathic understanding I have been describing is at its most effective at times of impasse, when the work is unproductive or grindingly slow, or when there is overt conflict that is not productive because something deeper has not been understood. Generally, though, treatment is successful to the degree to which the therapist's understanding derives from a sympathetic merger with the patient's position, no matter how hateful or perverse that place might initially seem.

Notes

1. An earlier version of this paper was given in October 2000 to members of The Foundation for Psychotherapy and Counselling on a post-qualifying course entitled "Regarding Difference".

CHAPTER FIVE

Thinking without the object: some deformations of the life of the mind brought about by maternal absence

Bernardine Bishop

E ssential to Bion's account of the development of thinking is the external fact of the present and returning breast (Bion, 1967b, pp. 110–119). That fact is taken for granted throughout this now classic theory. The external disappearance of the breast is not in the story. The breast comes and goes, and may come less and go more than the infant would like, but essentially the breast is present and returning.

In its regular and repeated absences the infant undergoes need-of-the-breast. That need has the character at times of pain, frustration, rage and desperation, described by Bion in terms of invasion by a bad object rather than as felt absence of a good and needed one; for absence is at this stage not apprehensible as a psychic reality. Absence is presence of the bad and attack by it. Thus, initially, the return of the breast means relief from the onslaught of that bad breast more than it means joy at incorporating the good one (Bion, 1962b, pp. 55–58).

Then, over time, with increasing maturity, things change. The unavailable breast changes in meaning. It can begin to be known as an absent good. The breast no longer mutates in absence into a negative presence. Instead, something like missing can begin, and, with it, something like introjection. What is not here now—not here yet—can still be known. It can be loved. The breast begins to be able to sustain the character internally, in its absence, that it has when present: the character that makes it that which is wanted. Absence, painful but tolerable, constitutes the ground of what will become thought. In an atmosphere of longing and hope, absence is what enables the rudiments of symbolization. Absence tolerated gives the self a chance to experience being alone, being a self. It prompts the first stirrings of memory, imagination, desire, learning, self-control and suffering. Absence, always within the context of presence, offers assurance that the self is able to continue to be through times of adversity, and proof that the feeling that it is dying can be survived and recovered from. Gradually, and not easily, the wind comes to be set fair for the sort of free and unfettered exploration of everything and anything, not without pain, but without paralysis, that the luckier ones amongst us call our thinking.

I am setting out these extremely familiar stages of growth towards thought in the Bionian model to bring to mind how absolutely their successful process depends on the ongoing presence and regular return of the external object. Without this presence and return, what we call the object—the good object, the breast—has no hope of becoming securely installed internally. Absence is only constructive of a capacity to experience being a self if it does not go on too long. What it arouses must be allayed—regularly and reliably. And at this stage that can only happen from outside. If absence degenerates into loneliness and terror something different will begin to happen. We think of Winnicott's, x, $x+y$, $x+y+z$ (Winnicott, 1980, p. 114). And if the sense of abandonment turns out to be true, that is, if the external object really does not externally return, then we are in territory not provided for by the theory of the development of thinking many of us take for granted.

And there are many reasons why this can happen, and we hear about quite a few of them from our patients. It does not have to be the mother's sudden death, though it can be. It can be her hospitalization or her love-affair or her lecture tour or a break-up of the family. Her disappearance does not have to be actually permanent, but the point reached in the infant is the one where the sense of her return, with the implications of that for internal structure-building, has been destroyed.

The children and the adults that $x + y + z$ infants become may not be unable to think, in the everyday sense, as understood by, say, their teachers, colleagues, perhaps patients. But it is only logical to suppose that the path to thinking each one of them has taken must be very different from what Bion is indicating to us as the proper inception of thought. The inference is inescapable that an internal world in which thought can happen is an internal world in which the good object has been securely introjected, and can thereafter be taken for granted at the core of the structure of the personality, something not sought, nor thanked, nor considered, but constituting the ground of our being.

It is one thing to understand the necessity of an internal good object, securely introjected, for the fullness of psychic and emotional life. But the internal good object is also specifically necessary to thought. Perhaps it may be argued that it is only in the context of the presence of the good object that pain can be borne, and the more pain can be borne the more freely we can think. The more we are warding off pain, the less we can think.

But of course—obviously—thinking is going to happen in some form or other when there is no good object. If rupture with the mother in the external world has been such that the good object has not been installed in the internal world, mental life does not die. But it may be that what has not been able to happen remains inexorably at the heart of the personality. It constitutes so catastrophic a lack, so central a sense that what should be there is not there, that the mind thereafter takes as its prime task—fundamentally as its only task—the rectification of that lack. That task will remain, I suggest, the unconscious psychic priority so long as it is not fulfilled. To put it another way, the deprived personality declares a state of emergency and enlists the mind, along with any other energies and resources it can lay hands on, to bring about in fantasy the return that never happened in fact, or to deny the disappearance that did. This project, which may be essential first-aid to psychic survival, causes, I suggest, severe and lasting deformation of the mind.

I often try to hear whether the patient I am listening to began their thinking in the freedom and openness which is enabled by an internal good object or whether they began it somewhere else. There is a palpable difference. It is the difference between someone who, never mind how many other problems they may have, is able to let their mind be, and someone who has adapted their mind, along with anything else available including the transference, to make themself feel different: better. Often when the mind is used, customized, in this way, to try to administer a feeling to the self, you can discern in the background the shadowy presence and overarching shape of the central project I have been describing—to effect the return that did not happen or make good the disappearance that did.

A pause in what is being said in a session may be a thinking pause, where the patient is able to go on thinking until he speaks again. But it often is not, of course, even when it appears or is intended to appear to be so. One may not be listening to someone whose thinking can quietly maintain itself, sustained all along by internalized return. It may be that at that moment in the session— the moment of the pause—something has gone wrong for the patient in his relationship with an object, which suddenly feels as if might disappear. In that case, immediate action will now be taken, evasive action, to avoid what may be felt as the hot breath of the affect of the original trauma. The situation is much too dangerous to think about, let alone share, and anyway words have never been there. What is threatened is his internal contact with his good object. This is not really a good object at all, but a deserting one; but none the less all-important to him. After a short silence, a patient I am getting to know starts again with something like: "I'm thinking of what you said about..." Am I hearing a thought, after a reflective silence, which has been able to use a thought of mine? Perhaps. But perhaps I am picking up a hint that there is an object which can suddenly abscond, an object which for that reason had better quickly be acknowledged and propitiated—"what you said". Am I hearing that object being politely cajoled to return? If so, it is possible that this patient does not have the freedom to use his mind to explore what he thinks is interesting and true, but, primarily and habitually, to keep his object. What I am calling deformations may be becoming apparent.

There is a moment in *Middlemarch* when Lydgate is thinking deeply and happily about his ideas. "In his dark eyes ... there was that placidity which comes from the fullness of contemplative thought—the mind not searching, but beholding..." (Eliot, 1994, p. 457). The mind not searching, but beholding. To be able to behold, a mind has to be open, to enjoy its freedom, to tolerate mysteries, contraries, the unexpected, uncertainties, darkness, not knowing. This must be the frame of mind Bion means when he says that thoughts pre-exist thinking, and thinking exists to deal with them (Bion, 1967b, pp. 110–111). To behold entails the internal presence of the good object.

The title of this paper is "Thinking without the object". The "without" of the title is intended to convey both without as the opposite of *with*, and without as the opposite of *within*. To behold is made possible by the enduring presence and availability of the good object—this is the object to think with. The object to think within implies a sense of the infinite capacities of the object to contain chaos and render it thinkable.

Where premature loss means thinking has come on stream without the object—in both senses—the mind will know a lot about searching, but I am arguing that it will not be able to behold. The power or entity that resides in that personality in the place of the good object is inevitably an object imbued with that early desertion This object holds the locus and has the status within the self of the good object, but lacks qualities essential to that goodness. It does not have what Ron Britton calls "that vital quality of the good mother of infancy of returning unsummoned and unmerited, of an object that transcends expectation, belief and justice" (Britton, 1998a, p. 140).

So we are thinking about a personality in which the good object is not a good object. But it is not no object; it is an introjected desired and deserting one. Some people who have not introjected a good object may opt for some sort of sufficiency without it—a schizoid solution, perhaps. Thinking may then take on a different colouring, perhaps move for preference towards the abstract and impersonal. But for those under consideration here the wound remains open, as it were, life-long, if the right things for them do not happen. It may be evident to them as infants that they can not live without the good object, and because what they have been offered is a deserting one, that is what they introject and have to try to keep good.

The emphasis here is on the implications of all this for the life of the mind, rather than on the emotional havoc; on the deformation of the life of the mind the emotional havoc brings about. This divides into two broad areas. In one the psychic effort seems to be focused more on effecting a return that did not happen, and in the other, on denying the disappearance that did, and disavowing the implications of that for the object's goodness. Why an infant chooses one defence rather than another we do not know. In any event, these two areas are not nearly so distinct as they are rendered here the sake of clarity.

The first is a condition already suggested, which is dominated by the return that did not really happen. Winnicott's "Fear of breakdown" (Winnicott, 1980) postulates that something which happened in infancy, but has not been subjectively experienced because of the rudimentary nature of the psyche at the time, is placed in the future and feared. In what is being considered here, the trauma is placed in the future and feared, but, further, there is a fantasy that it may be averted. What is sought is the emotion of relief proper to the return. What the mind adapts thinking to seek for the self is something like a huge, epiphanic sigh of relief.

This is not the natural life of thought. It reminds me somewhat of the unnatural practices we use in farming. In the natural existence of, say, a hen, she has all sorts of possibilities and varieties of mobility and shades of activity. In a battery, she is modified into an egg-laying machine. Thought can bring relief, as a hen can lay an egg; but that is not all either can do or wants to do in a state of nature. Where the personality structure described here obtains, thoughts large and small have the marks of one compass-setting, which is orientated steadily and life-long away from that early waiting-in-vain, and towards the provision of psychic equivalents of intimations of return.

I had a patient many years ago whose father told her later—she was grownup and the mother had died—that the mother had left the family when my patient was 4 months old, and had returned a year later, my patient now 16 months. This year, never talked about at the time, lost to her memory but omnipresent in her experience, had set a prevailing wind that affected not only her emotional life and relationships but the very grain of her thinking. She liked fixed opinions, explanations, attitudes that did not change, unquestioned beliefs, and seemed at first to hop from one to another, as if what was inbetween was too dangerous. Landing safely from a hop on the dry land of another known point of view offered a tiny dose of the relief she was always trying to procure in full measure. Uncertainty must be avoided, waiting was intolerable, beholding out of the question. I was impressed as often by the resourcefulness and ingenuity of defensive structures, the will-to-live, and will-to-love, that they express, when you think of the enormity of what was kept at bay in a sudden and unmediated loss on that scale. Return had never happened—psychically, another woman came back—but the lonely hope of it had endured, and did still, shown in all sorts of ways, some of them pathological.

I mentioned danger—danger of the unknown ground between the fixed beliefs. I suspect that in this order of infantile psychic predicament all thinking is dangerous, unless, as another early-left patient says, you know exactly where it is going to lead. Thinking is dangerous because the infant believes that in his omnipotence he has banished the breast, and he does not know what in his emerging self has had that effect. Could it have been his thinking? If so, the mind itself becomes an object of dread. No wonder it is harnessed to bring about mental experiences that feel like moments of return, not thoughts that explore. Or behold.

Another patient with a chequered first year found it difficult to be sure that the front door was locked at night and the gas taps turned off etc. There are so many ways of considering this sort of anxiety, but I found myself thinking about it, with this particular person, amongst other approaches, in terms of the project to engineer the moments of return. When the task finally felt done there was a sigh of relief, small, perhaps, but again, not so small, in that it partook qualitatively of the sigh of relief that was waited for and had never happened. There were also more purely mental manifestations of this. Phobic of memory loss, she would ruminate endlessly over some forgotten detail of no intrinsic importance to her, and if she could get it back, which was all that mattered to her about it, there would be the sense of return and the sigh of relief. The thinking she brought to the work she did for a living had a high degree of solution-hunting in it, appropriate to the matter in hand, but subjectively having its own private source.

In these cases we see knowing, which is only one of the aims of thinking, becoming overvalued at the expense of others. If uncertainty and suspense have grown too intense, not remedied by return, inner resources are ransacked for any antidote to that unbearable helplessness. The craving for certainty, as that antidote, becomes so pressing that it deforms the mind.

A word now about a possible sidelight on the aetiology of obsessional and phobic disorders. Disorders of terror. If alpha function, provided by the mother and her breast, is the dynamic process which metabolizes beta elements into the dreamable and the thinkable, its absence must make something different happen to beta elements. Perhaps one of the things that can happen is that, unable to be detoxified, and generating psychotic terror, they are bound, piecemeal, into what become obsessional and phobic symptoms. Some narrative and sense is given them, but it is not anywhere near common sense, one of the properties of alpha function. "If I have not washed my hands enough a germ from there may get on to there... So I had better throw the whole casserole I am cooking away." The beta flavour is addressed and to some extent managed by pseudo-reason and pseudo-science, sequences of cause and effect which seem to the sufferer to have unanswerable logic. G.K. Chesterton wrote that a madman does not usually seem to be someone who has lost his reason, but someone who has lost everything except his reason (Chesterton, 1999, pp. 12–22). These mental processes indeed travesty and in a way parody thinking, and in affect are full of nightmare that cannot be dreamt. They offer insight into what can happen to thinking without the object.

The second broad area of emphasis I am taking is where the mother's disappearance is denied and/or the implications of that disappearance for her goodness are disavowed. Imagine that an object which cannot be trusted is becoming installed at the heart of the self, where the good object belongs for the fortunate. Meanwhile it is of absolute importance to the life and growth of the self that the object should be good, should be honest, should be trustworthy. This is an existential dilemma of the greatest possible urgency for the infant. How he responds to it will affect the rest of his life. The self-sufficient solution, as I have called it, seems to be an option for some infants. One early-left patient, when he began to sense the presence of, and therefore for him simultaneously the desertion by, the breast in the transference, had a dream that he was curled in a hoop, sucking his penis. Perhaps a lot of infants would seek this solution if they could, but they cannot; the drive to love and be loved is too strong.

Indeed we must put the issue of love at the heart of the discussion, for that is where it belongs. For the early left the question too painful to ask is: "Does she love me?" The answer to that question, by hook or by crook, has to be "Yes", or life cannot go on. With Ron Britton's good mother of infancy, and all the other ordinary devoted mothers, the love question never even has to be raised. In that setting, the loving and reliable qualities of the mother are trusted and taken for granted. They can be introjected in time, and processes of separation can begin. Eventually she can be external, and gradually begin to be perceived something like the person she objectively is. More than that, the internal object that reflects her and that we call the good object, constituting the core of the personality, can be allowed its own proper freedom and trusted spontaneity within. But the infants we are talking about are the ones for whom this process stopped in its tracks. For these latter, the way is now clear for the narcissistic solution. We enter the world of the idealized good object. I am keeping the word "good" for the object, although "idealized" contradicts that goodness, to indicate the tension and strain on the infant. He needs the object to be good, and from now on must exert himself to keep it so, in order that the all-important answer to the love question—"Does she love me?"—should be "Yes".

Central to the narcissistic solution is the fact that the object comes under the sway of infantile narcissistic omnipotence. This is so in the internal world. And when the object is projected, that is the mode of the relationship. That is the character of the transference. But something we have to remember is that what is safeguarded, however ineptly, is the patient's desperately beleaguered need to love and be loved. I often think we forget that poor Narcissus did actually think it was someone else he was seeing in the water.

One of the deep configurations of narcissistic love is the secret sense of being the favourite. If there is an unconscious belief, a belief that is kept unconscious because it cannot be faced, that the answer to the love question is "No, she hates me", a defensive counter-belief, in Ron Britton's language, may come on stream (Britton, 1998a, p. 16). The counter-belief holds that "Yes, she loves me, and we were torn apart as much against her will as mine." In this case self and object are a secretly faithful and star-crossed pair of lovers, and this may become the basis of the transference relationship. A hint of this may be evident when a patient says a sentence beginning something like: "Are you *allowed* to tell me...?" The boundariless relationship we both want is being dutifully sacrificed to priorities outside our control. It is one of the strengths of the analytic setting that it can lend itself to this projection, without which the underlying fantasies would not be reached and resolved.

This internal relationship of self and object survives from the time when there were only two people in the world. It is a stark, primitive, dualistic world, a paranoid–schizoid world—only two people, and if not love, then hate. But the enormous difficulty in giving up this archaic relationship of self and object is that it dates from the time when it was a matter of survival to answer the love question with a "Yes". It takes a long time and much experience of therapy, as we all know, for a new possibility to emerge, a greater variety of colours. "It doesn't mean you hate me if you don't love only me"—that brave new world is still a long way off. There are some therapies that never recover from the therapist's too cavalier response to this struggle.

In this paradigm, we see writ large something very important about the phenomenon of narcissistic love. It is potentially catastrophic if the object is different from what I think it is. For some early-left patients, and some others too, there is a very short and steep skid row, within any session, from the sense that the therapist is doing or saying something wrong—wrong, meaning out of keeping with the object of narcissistic possession—to the utter destitution and loneliness of the early trauma. Part of this at least may be because whatever was going on in the mind of the mother to make her disappear must have been going on in her before she went. The only sure safeguard against this disastrous state of affairs is that the therapist should not have a separate inside of his own at all. "You only think the thoughts I know you think!" This is problematic to freedom in the analytic work, as we know, for both patient and therapist. More difficult still is the predicament that arises when the patient suspects the therapist of responses the therapist may not know he has. "You may think you didn't mean to be cruel to me, but what if you did mean to, unconsciously?" The object which does not know its own heart, supposing the risk has been taken of allowing it one, may reflect a disjunction between what the mother's presence and breast had seemed to promise and what actually happened.

It is inevitable that the therapist's departure from script causes recurrence of the original, raw, infantile agony, and only gradually and painfully will things be able to be contained, understood and changed. Another problem, of course, is that if I own you, omnipotently, as my narcissistic object, much though I love and admire you, I will also despise you, because you are my invention, and of the two of us, only I have life. As in William Blake's poem, where the loved one is netted with silk and caged in gold:

> He loves to sit and hear me sing
> Then, laughing, sports and plays with me;
> Then stretches out my golden wing
> And mocks my loss of liberty.
> [*Song: How Sweet I Roamed*, p. 26 of 1977 edn.]

The narcissistic love-object can be idolized and idealized, but not accorded a free and separate life. Like Desdemona. The notion of the object's really having a mind of its own in which unknown things are happening touches too nearly on the early desertion. The object's freedom is equivalent, psychically, to being rejected by it. So the object's private and spontaneous life must be eliminated.

At an extreme end of what is the same continuum, the murderer Dennis Nilsen propped up the corpses of his victims to watch television with him and, later, when asked why he had killed, said "For company." A very stark statement that aliveness equals desertion. The only good object is a dead object.

If there is no object into which the infant can project, or if the object disappears, one defensive strategy for the infant may be to take its own body as container. Jennifer Silverstone refers to this in her essay in this volume. This may lead to psychosomatic disorders and eating problems. A further possibility is that it may lead to hypochondria. Bernd Nissen (Nissen, 2000) finds a correlation between hypochondria and what he calls "Severe, real, separation-related trauma in the relationship with the mother."

To attempt an aetiology: let us postulate that in the sudden and traumatic severance from the mother, and in the absence of adequate mediation of this by anyone else, an infant unconsciously substitutes his own body for the meaning of hers. [Possibly, from another angle, this could be viewed along the lines of the model famously described by Donald Meltzer (Meltzer, 1966) as a move towards possessive intrusion into the mother.] Thus the infant's own body, with its mysterious life, vital to the preservation of the self, mutates entirely inappropriately into his vehicle for the meaning of the good object. As we have seen, the object occupying the position of trust proper to the good object is not in fact in his case good at all, and risks at any moment being unmasked. It cannot be good, for it has been all too plainly demonstrated as unreliable, and that unreliability has in consequence become part of its very nature. It follows that the object now represented by the body is both greatly overcathected in the demands on it that it should be and remain good, and at the same time profoundly feared as capricious, suspect and dangerous, even malignant. The object's goodness, like that of the body, may be only skin deep. There is no infrastructure for that unconscious hope of its looking after its own goodness in its own uncontrollable but trustworthy way. The object the body carries is the one which somewhere inside itself, invisibly for the moment, is cooking up a plan which has the psychic meaning of a sentence of death for the infant. A dire situation, for the body now is not what a body should be in the integrity of a self, and is conscripted to be an arena in which battles between terrible doubts of, and the search for reassurance about, the goodness of the object are fought. Thus hypochondria. Thus also, it seems likely, further problems for the life of the mind stemming from so profound a deformation of an embodied self.

I want to say something about thinking without the object that perhaps one could call thinking within the idealized object. It refers to the question of discipleship. First to describe the unexceptionable version of this. It must be a wise and truth-seeking activity of the mind to like what someone is saying, or what they are like, and to want to learn from them. Identity is made up of these sorts of identifications. You might even come under the influence of such a person, choose. a life's work because of that; and this might also be helpful to personal growth. Then you might find more of your own voice, agree to differ, and move on to another way of developing, perhaps to another person's influence, perhaps not, building on what you have. These are pictures of healthy dependency. They are not available within the psychic structures we are considering, which deny and cannot risk dependency. Suppose it is the idealized object of the narcissistic love-relationship that is projected on to the other person. Then it will be very difficult to bear being different from them: differing. Obviously, because in the narcissistic world it is taken for granted that only that which is like can be loved. As the object is omnipotently controlled by the self to be thus and not other than thus, so, it is assumed, the object needs omnipotently to control the self. In the narcissistic world the object is narcissistic. It will love what is like itself and cast a cold eye on what is not.

In the transference this creates special problems. I think of a patient who thought she had good reason to believe that her therapist belonged to his local Labour Party. This sparked a great interest in the history and development of the Labour Party, and attempts to draw the therapist, in order to be the same as him, on what he thinks of the way the Labour Party has gone now. As the patient gradually became able to think about this, rather than enacting it, she realized to her surprise that she could not tell whether she was genuinely interested in the Labour Party or whether she was only interested in feeling at one with her therapist. Imitation, stemming from the narcissistic infrastructure, and need to intrude into the object, or identification pointing the way to true identity?

A problem arises for the freedom of the life of the mind if it is more important to be like the transferential object than to behold the mind's own original thoughts in truthfulness. On the larger scale, as we know too well, a demagogue can use this, and bring about in otherwise apparently sensible people a passionate preference for his approval, oneness with him, over their own truth. In terms of the early-left, perhaps we touch again on the question of what, in the infant's psychic reality, detonated the desertion on him. Was it— *could* it have been?—that he had an emergent, separate self of his own? Was that an outrage on the object for which he was repudiated?

We must not underestimate the complexity of these questions of identification and identity. What looks like narcissistic incorporation may turn out to be the beginnings of healthy discipleship. A lot of us may remember something relevant about how we began to want to train as psychotherapists, which may not have been entirely pathological. Perhaps the young woman really was interested in the Labour Party. Otherwise, why didn't quite a different formative myth arrange itself in her mind around her therapist,—that he restored mediaeval paintings in his spare time, or had his heart in Friends of the Earth? Are we unconsciously drawn to discipleships which reflect or adumbrate our true selves? Is what looks like a narcissistic entanglement sometimes in fact a way out of one?

The way out of the narcissistic entanglement has to include the presence of a good enough and reliable enough outside object. The personality in its deepest layers is still fixed at the point where we came in—where it can only find, or, in the first place, be found by, what it needs outside itself. If a good enough outside object can be found in the person of the therapist, these breath-taking risks may begin to be possible. Recovery of the mind as well as of the emotions, if the two are separable, may come about.

A particular hurdle is reached if the capacity to introject is not, as it were, in cold storage, but turns out to be actually defective. I have encountered this in a patient whose mother was psychotic. This patient was early-left, not in the physical, but in a mental and emotional sense. I have tried to confine my discussion to the problems of gross maternal absence, something more clearcut than a mostly present and returning mother's inability to keep her infant adequately in mind. But there is a continuum, and disappearance is only the extreme and material version. In a real sense, this patient was not early-left, which expression presupposes a different time beforehand, something to lose. She never knew a sane mother. As I have come to see it, it was terribly important for her, as a life-or-death measure, to render non- operational her introjective faculty. Again, I am awed by the sure-footedness of early defences. If she had been able to introject, it seems clear that she would have introjected the psychosis. From later developments this becomes probable: her mother desperately wanted her to share the florid delusional life, and resented her not doing so. Much must happen if she is to be able to reverse this long-ago, life- saving, lonely decomissioning of a vital part of the self.

It seems appropriate to end by quoting a verse of a poem by Elizabeth Jennings an early-left patient found during a break. It is about absence, which takes us back to the beginning of this paper, and about starting to be able to bear suffering and be sustained through it; and about hard-won love and trust in an external object.

Your absence has been stronger than all pain,
And I am glad to find that when most weak
Always my mind returned to you again.
Through all the noisy nights, when, harsh awake,
I longed for day and light to break—
In that harsh desert, you were life, were rain.

[Jennings, 1986, p. 78]

CHAPTER SIX

An absence of mind

Jennifer Silverstone

T his paper is an attempt to understand autistic and false-self states through both the body and the mind. My thesis will be that where there is an absence in the mother's internal world of the baby in her mind, the identity of the baby becomes vulnerable both in the mind of the mother and in the mind of the child. The absence of thought about and around the baby both in the internal world and later in external reality can produce a state of mind where thinking is experienced as dangerous in the developing child. The body thus becomes a form of expression and a defence against thinking and somatizing in various forms takes on the possibility of a deeper meaning. The sensations of the body are concretized and can become a means of expressing the unbearable. Sensation replaces thought and can be seen as a defence against thinking. The body becomes a metaphor for the whole self. The self as a thinking self is hidden and defended against by the capacity of the body to distract the mind.

I will be linking two main areas of thinking.

The first section focuses on what happens in the mind of the child that contributes to the creation of a false self and a lack of authenticity, and how that falseness and lack of authenticity is experienced in the psychotherapeutic work. I shall be concerned here especially with the patient's narrative of the family story; and with what it might mean to talk about the idea the mother has in her mind of what the baby is for her, who the baby will be, and what the baby will be. This concern also involves a focus on her relationship with the idea of a baby, how this develops in her mind, how this changes when there is a live baby, and how the baby in the mind of the mother relates to the mother in the mind of baby.

I am also interested in exploring the triadic relationship—how the child/baby is incorporated into the minds of the couple, and then how the idea of the couple rests in the mind of the child and in the adult. I am also interested in and will speak about the notion of gender and gender identification and how that might be a disturbance to the mother and the father who in the expectation of having a male or female child lose an ungendered, undifferentiated baby. I shall claim that this early undifferentiated harmony is a precursor to the capacity to rest in the self and to experience an integration of thought and feeling which enables us to tolerate and may help us to understand the later difficulties of life.

The second section focuses on the part the body plays as a defence against feeling and how the body is experienced and contained. In an attempt to understand some somatic symptoms, I shall consider some eating disorders, and the features, which I call autistic because of their rigid and defensive structure, that are concrete attempts to hold on to the body whilst keeping the mind clear of thought. I shall illustrate these states with clinical material.

Although eating disorders have been variously discussed in terms of body distortion I shall be concentrating on eating as an attack on thinking and on the meaning of its regressive orality. Eating in a disordered way empties the mind of its objects and allows for the body to become the focus of sensation. I shall argue that some bodily sensations are regressive, and emerge as an attempt to rework the sensations and merging of an infant. These sensations link with autistic features, when words or sensations in mind and body are held on to in a similar way to external objects—this can be understood as an attempt to free the mind from thought and shift the body into focus. I shall illustrate how the empty mind of the mother and the then empty mind of the child are mediated by food and feeding.

Section one: the patient's narrative

A patient coming into therapy is invited to tell a story, the story of his or her life, describing how they got to the point of seeking the therapeutic relationship. Telling the story, the narrative structure and the way it is told sets the frame for a preliminary under-standing, and that understanding along with transference feelings sets the stage, the context for therapeutic work. A life has in some way or another a beginning, a middle, and a phantasized end. Some patients start the story in the middle in the crisis of the moment; others trail back to stories within stories, and mythic structures of how their lives began. Being human, others are needed to explain their existence, for as Winnicott patiently pointed out "there is no such thing as a baby". Some narratives are bleached of others, setting the patient alone centre stage, others feel that the "other" defined them by placing them in the context of being unwanted, unexpected, arrived too soon, disposed of too early. Some feel they were not what was wanted, or indeed who was wanted, and so a selfhood at its moment of emergence was in question. Then there are those who have been created to be everything for everyone, or someone, to fill a gap, to replace a dead other, to heal a mourning, or to create a new dawn.

These stories and their recounting take shape in the setting of the consulting room and they come to rest in the therapist's mind. The therapist becomes the container of the narrative, the mother who can remember the vicissitudes of how it is to get to the place that one speaks from, the mother who can hold onto memory without fear. Birth and conception stories sometimes emerge; these too can provide a rich seam of understanding. Miss A for example was conceived after many miscarriages and was born when the mother was tired of the process of imagining, and though she consciously "wanted a child" she seemed to have had no more mental space for a baby as a living and demanding separate being. This absence of being imagined in the mind has haunted our work together with the transference being elusive and contact of a deep mind to mind connection taking place rarely. Mother had no mind for the baby and when the baby cried she fed her, over and over again right through to a steady obesity. André Green speaks eloquently of aspects of this lack of holding of the infant in the mind of the mother in his paper "The dead mother". Here he elaborates on the kind of depression that he meets in patients who have an experience of a real live mother but a mother who is experienced as "dead", that is absent in her mind through bereavement. He makes a moving and clear case for a distinction between the experience of actual loss of the mother and the phantasied loss of an object. "It does not concern the loss of a real object ... the essential characteristic of this depression is that it takes place in the presence of the object, which is itself absorbed by a bereavement" (André Green in Kohon, 1999, p. 149).

As psychotherapists we are now informed in our work not only by object relations theorists, but also by the work done by Colin Trevarthen and Daniel Stern who have researched and written about the earliest observations that take place between mothers and their infants. Here we have bodies of work detailing the earliest connectedness between an infant and the caring other. Alongside this come the infant observation studies based on the work of Ester Bick and the new theories of mind of Fonagy and Moran.

In his paper "Thinking about thinking" Peter Fonagy writes about the treatment of borderline or near borderline patients and the analyst's capacity to hold on to their own mind and mental functioning being central to the therapeutic work. "If the therapist's mentalizing capacity is used by the patient to support and maintain his identity, the patient's dependence upon the therapist for maintaining a relatively stable mental representation of himself will be absolute" (Fonagy, 1991, p. 42). I am focusing in this paper on less dramatic and total absences of mind in the mother but I am making a similar case for the therapist's capacity to maintain their own vitality and sense of self and its position in the work. The disturbances of mind in the adult patients I am talking about can be traced back to the mind of the mother, and sometimes to the collective minds of the parental couple. This absence of mind in the mother has an impact both on the developing mind of the child and subsequently on and in the mind of the adult.

The baby needs the mother in many ways. The object mother and the environment mother, the good enough mother who does not over-anticipate or move too far ahead of the infant and therefore pre-empt experience and become a false but perfect mother, a mother who can tolerate and process through her own functioning mind the distress of the other. In order to create these periods of harmony with the baby she must have a mind that is available to accept the baby's primitive hopes and fears, infantile terrors and ecstasies. In other words she has to be able to accept and to process projections and re-introject and mirror the intimate and subtle connections, which are part of the capacity to become a harmonious couple.

In the face of the absence of the part of the mind in the mother that is attached to the mind of the baby the baby has to find ways of imagining and tolerating his primitive states of mind without the containing mind of an other. It may be that the mother cannot conceptualize the baby as having a mind of its own and the baby is then forced to rely on its own developing mind and on its own developing resources of containment and on finding ways of catching the mother's attention in order to develop and thrive. In periods of the absence of mind in the mother the baby learns, as it were, to defend itself against this primitive loss and an absence of this mutuality of thinking. The baby will learn to defend itself against this loss in many ways.

The mother is both the container for her infant's projections and the processor of them; if this function is lacking through an absence of this process within her mind the baby is forced to turn in on itself. The mother also functions as the mirror for the infant reflecting the inner world of both their minds as well as fragments of outer reality. She has to be able to respond to the idea of her infant developing a capacity to think and to produce traces of primitive thoughts that can ultimately be re-introjected. Before this can be achieved, and an achievement it is, there has to be the idea, a paradoxical one, that there is a space within the mother to allow for mental merging, a taken for granted concept in the baby. The patient who is devoted to understanding, by every possible nuance, the state of mind of the therapist is signalling that this watching and intuiting comes from the earliest attempts at merging, introjecting and re-introjecting what is happening in mother's mind. An absence of mind pushes the infant into attempting to understand the other in an attempt to understand the self. The baby is in a frequent merged state with its mother. "To the infant, its mother and itself make up one whole person. Mother is not yet a distinct object for her nurseling, but at the same time she is something much vaster than simply another human being. She is a total environment..." (McDougal, 1989, p. 33).

I am looking at this space where there is an absence of mind, and thinking about it in relation to the formation of two particular concepts, the false self and what I am calling autistic features. This is not to say that there are no other defensive structures and useful ones to explore, and indeed the early environment is a breeding ground for borderline states. The link between false-self and autistic features is that they both emanate from similar early disturbances in the mind of the mother; therefore in the counter-transference there is a similar difficulty in holding onto the capacity to think in an authentic and spontaneous way. There is a controversy around the definition of autism between the organicist view and the view of autism as a psychological deficit. Nowhere is this better explored than in Anne Alvarez's *Live Company*. Here she explores the notion of multiple causation, calling on the work of Tustin, Meltzer et al. Summarising the controversy Alvarez states:

> ...organic factors can lead to the same external appearance as psychogenic factors ... I would add, for example that a baby with mild dysfunction and a limp and flaccid or disorganised approach to life, born to an already depressed mother whose depression worsens at her failure to cope with her apathetic baby, may then become even less engaged, producing more depression in the mother. And so on ... No neurological impairment at all in a baby with all the normal readiness to engage in relationships might be met with depression or withdrawal in the mother to such a severe degree that the baby may reluctantly but slowly and surely give up trying to engage her attention, with devastating implications for his emotional and cognitive development. [Alvarez, 1992, p. 186]

I am saying then that the false self, as Winnicott describes it, is a configuration which can be formed from an adaptation in the baby to his experience of not being considered as authentic and individual within his mother's mind—"the mother who is not good enough is not able to implement the infant's omnipotence, and so she repeatedly fails to meet the infant gesture; instead she substitutes her own gesture which is to be given sense by the compliance of the infant" (Winnicott, 1965, p. 145). The infant very early on in its life has the capacity to engage the mother in a false way, losing the spontaneity and genuine joy of being found for himself. It is not uncommon to hear patients refer to themselves as one of many, not special or different from any other patient who is arriving regularly, on time, and possibly burdening the therapist with similar problems. In the transference the feelings can be deadening and the lack of a capacity for genuine empathy in meeting the patient in laughter or grief can be experienced as frightening and indeed alienating. Daniel Stern, in describing what he calls attunement behaviour, and what others may call early mirroring, between mother and baby, suggests that:

> parents inevitably exert some degree of selective bias in their attunement behaviours, and in doing so they create a template for the infant's shareable interpersonal world. This applies to all internal states ... And this is clearly how the "false self" can begin—by utilising that portion of inner experience that can achieve intersubjective acceptance with the inner experience of the other, at the expense of the remaining, equally legitimate, portions of inner experience. [Green, 1999, p. 210]

It is therefore paradoxical that with patients such as these, following the material with empathic response and interpretation is not enough, and in some senses is too much for the patient to bear. For these patients, who are holding on to a compliant part of the self, are waiting to be found in the trueness of themselves and waiting to test the analytic water with a genuine gesture of selfhood. The patient needs the therapist's mind to create the potential space for internal acceptance and aliveness. Some of these patients express their inner worlds as dead and flat and without imagination, and indeed the imaginative gesture, sometimes the ability to come to a session a few minutes late or to disagree with a therapeutic intervention is a sign that there are two minds at work in the room. Compliance precludes authentic mental intercourse.

Christopher Bollas, writing about a patient with what appeared to be an absence of mind, and filling the sessions with repeated empty silences, says:

> We could say that through a subtle form of regression within the transference he was giving up some of his inner self states to the other who used mind to help sort out the feelings and to reflect usefully upon lived experience. To my way of thinking this was the analysand's symbolic return to the mother who had not been there for him in the earliest months of life. [Bollas, 1995, p. 101]

So far I have not included father or "an other" in this discussion, but I have referred to the idea of the couple and its place in the narrative of the patient's life. A couple after all is needed, despite the mediation of a test tube, to create a baby. The idea of the couple in the mind of the mother can protect and enliven the idea about the baby both in imagination and in reality. Some babies have two minds to play with where there is a sense of couple in mother's mind. Some mothers have access to the mind of the father, who in turn is holding his infant in mind; this enables a shared sense of holding the baby in the mind of the couple. In other words the mother may sometimes hold the baby in mind as long as she is holding it within the consciousness of a two-person relationship. Other mothers deep in maternal preoccupation are unaware of the place of others in the mind of the baby; the baby exists only for them. The point I wish to make is that the emergence of the idea of a couple in the patient's mind may well work in favour of the analytic intervention.

Ron Britton sees the development of and the tolerance for what he calls triangulation, the capacity of an individual to develop a third position, as crucial in being able to formulate ideas around the difference between acquiring belief and gaining knowledge:

> Cognitive, scientific and cultural development is not simply the acquisition of new ideas but an act of emancipation from pre-existing beliefs. I suggest that this involves the bringing together of subjective experience with objective self-awareness so that one sees oneself in the act of believing something. This depends on internal triangulation, and that in turn requires the toleration of an internal version of the Oedipal situation. [Britton, 1998b, p. 13]

In other words there is a development in the mind of the infant that the couple are both inside in procreation, and outside in development of the two-person parental relationship.

Fathers present and represent difference, they cannot be mother but they can mother. The couple who produce a baby have, to my mind, a limited period but a vital one in which to relate to the newborn as an infant, a baby, a moment, which is gender-free. Gender is an imposition on the emerging self of the baby getting in between the experience of simply being a baby rather than having to become a boy or a girl child. It is at this time that a baby is free from preconceptions about a self, and free to be itself, a spontaneous moment of aliveness which we strive to repeat and look out for in the psychotherapeutic work.

So far I have talked about spontaneity, the ability to be authentic as the true self, which is the underbelly of the contrived static false construction achieved by the baby to appease and please an absent-minded mother. This state of affairs is of course a defence, a defence against being found. Being found is to be found wanting, and the dilemma for the patient is balancing a longing to be found for their essential self and a dread that once again it will not be recognized. This mechanism appears in its most raw form in infancy where in the midst of so many projections and interjections life, mind, body, and inner world begin to take on their inevitable shape:

> Long before birth, perhaps as early as fourteen weeks of gestation, the human infant can be said to manifest behaviour and to declare the fundamental qualities of its character ... as its ambience loses the ample dimensions of the early months and becomes restrictive, the foetus develops a yearning to recover its freedom and an expectation of another world from which it receives auditory clues. When it is strong enough it struggles to be free and succeeds ... the panic before the first breath is succeeded by the delicious expansion of the lungs; the explosion of noise becomes quickly modulated and delightfully musical; the initial chill is quickly countered; the blinding glare takes wondrous shape. But the mobile limbs have been bound down by a thousand gravitational cords, and the sense of helplessness, of being lost in limitless space, mobilizes the expectation of a saviour, and the mouth seeks it out and finds it. The infant's panicky fragmentation is pulled together by the mother's arms and her voice and smell, which are familiar; and the vast space is given a point of origin geometrically by this nipple-in-the-mouth. And when the eyes begin to see the mother's face and breast, and the flesh to feel the chain of desire, her eyes are the sanctuary in which the passionate yearning towards the beauty of this new world can find the reciprocity that makes it bearable. [Meltzer cited in Harris Williams & Waddell, 1991, p. xv]

This quote, itself abridged, comes from Donald Meltzer at his most poetic. He is encouraging us to identify with the infant in its earliest bodily states, a mass of undifferentiation, and putting into language the unspoken longing to be held in the gaze and the mind and arms of mother. He is, as I am, taking a position that the mother has a relationship with the undifferentiated infant as soon as she recognizes that conception has taken place, and there is a new embryonic life in her womb. He too eloquently expresses that even at this primitive, simple stage of development the baby receives sounds, sensations, and traces of what we might later call feelings from this primitive relationship with its mother. For it is very early on that thoughts and fantasies about the new born come to mother's mind, or the trauma or ambivalence of the pregnancy begin to deny the existence of a new life, even as it is beginning.

Section two: the body as a defence against feeling

I want to look now at the function of the body, and how the body holds the baby's external excitations and internal murmuring when there is a lack of maternal containment. When mother has a mind for the baby the soothing of the skin, the bathing of the body, the holding of the whole body, takes on a deeper meaning and enables the baby to have a sense of owning and enjoying its own body. When this bodily holding is successfully achieved it enables, paradoxically, an adult to have a body that is forgotten, rather than having a body that becomes a preoccupying force in adult life; the body and its demands are not then used a defence against thinking. "In the solitude of concentration the other object that disappears is the body. The good enough environment of the body can be taken for granted; it is most reliably present by virtue of its absence" (Phillips, 1993, p. 37).

Ester Bick, Dinora Pines, and others have written about the holding and symbolic function of the skin and the skin's somatic response to a lack of early maternal holding. So now I am looking at the baby's capacity for understanding and forming a relationship to its body which links with mother's capacity to hold the whole infant in her mind. The development of the false gesture enables the infant to produce for the mother an idea of the self while keeping the true self hidden—a defence against the fear of disappointing the mother. The false gesture, the lack of the internal capacity to hold the baby in the mind, leaves the breast in the paradoxical position of becoming both full and empty, internal and external, brought to mind as fulfilling or as hopelessly tantalizing.

The breast offered and used, loved and hated, frustrated and yearned for creates the psychic space for frustration, satiation, bliss, and thought. When frustration is tolerated, love and hate accomplished and not feared, the capacity for transitional space is created. For Winnicott and others, expressed in other language, the space between the mother and the breast is the space where creativity, to think for and of oneself and to live within a sense of having an imagination, emerges. If loss is too great, if frustration cannot be tolerated, false selves emerge falsely adapting to false sets of ideas which cannot take root deeply enough to be the precursor for internalized thought, and they come to rest as ideas at the periphery of internalization and await their fate to become projections.

In the merging of mind and body some of these false-self patients, though adept at disguise, still have to find ways of holding themselves together bodily. For the patient who was not allowed to cry, as crying represented failure for mother, passivity was induced by food, a full mouth then a full stomach induces sleep and silence in the baby and creates an illusion of contentment. For this patient, to want for anything material and concrete, to experience both desire and frustration internal or external in the here of now of life became an impossibility. An immediate and false solution had to be found, and the one that was embedded from infancy was the oral gratification and satiation of food, the preoccupation with the why and how of the taking in the food providing a disturbance to thought; an absence of mind and an activity which comes to end when sleep overtakes the body as it struggles to digest its load. This activity symbolized a belief in a false internal process and a link therefore to the absent-minded and anxiously silencing mother.

The more the baby ate the quieter it became leaving the adult out of touch with all bodily sensations of what it feels like to be physically full or empty. Baby, toddler, and adult right through the developmental hurdles that however painful enable psychic resolution of love, hate, pleasure, and pain are bypassed when the mind and thought are annexed to the constant chatter of bodily states and functions. The mind when troubled has to be fed symbolically, just as the mind of the anorexic has to be starved. The preoccupation with taking in, either in huge endless mouthfuls or in minute particles chewed repeatedly for the last vestiges of flavour, can be interpreted as an attempt to fill the mind with oral preoccupations; mouth, nipple, the un-thought feed from the absent mother; rather than with the painful thoughts that may involve the here and now of a life lived.

Maintaining body weight outside the boundaries of the ordinary takes enormous mental preoccupation, anorexics, bulimics, and overeaters are constantly filling their minds with their addictive behaviour and avoiding thought and connection with the other. Noticing body weight and appearance in a patient is often a moving and difficult moment, demanding the recognition of another thinking mind in the room. This can mobilize in the transference the wish for a repetition of the early undifferentiated merging, therefore wanting an unseeing mother therapist, whilst experiencing the simultaneous terror, excitement, and exposure of being truly seen in a clear and spontaneous way by a mother therapist who can hold the patient in her mind.

Another patient felt himself to be saved by the onset of migraine at around the age of six. Blinding him with pain and causing him to vomit he was invariably put to bed in sick bays of his various boarding schools—so creating for himself a sanctuary of recovery he would sleep until he recovered his sense of self. By the time he came into therapy he was breaking down with the pressure of the unspoken and unknown man he had become to himself, and he had a new set of somatic symptoms, a burning acidity in his gut, and what he called a public phobia, a fear that he could not speak.

Many babies hold themselves in their distress in physical ways, itching the skin, biting their fingers, pulling their hair, and banging, often rhythmically, their heads. In her paper, "Addiction to near-death", Joseph explores this bodily theme and adds to it the notion of "chuntering", a kind of constant internal monologue which can take the place of, stand in for, and move away from thought. "My impression is that these patients as infants, because of their pathology, have not just turned away from frustrations or jealousies or envies into a withdrawn state, nor have they been able to rage and yell at their objects. I think they have withdrawn into a secret world of violence..." (Joseph, 1989, p. 137). This is violence against the bodily self and with it comes bodily pain and a persuasive description of its addictive quality.

Though Betty Joseph's paper describes very severe pathology, the reworking of the infantile pain, the pain in the head, migraine, which may have been a vestige of the pain created by too much crying for mother to return, creates the illusion for the patient that he does not have to have another mind to relate to; the pain replaces the two-person connection, and he is unconsciously repeating the experience of not being held in mind by mother.

Being held in mind is a precursor to being thought about. Being thought about is the beginning of the formation of the capacity to think—we think for ourselves because we have been thought about in someone else's mind. Thinking is a route to feeling and feelings can be transformed into thought, beta elements and alpha functions in Bion's language. Absence of thought is characterized by nameless dread, falling forever, lack of containment. Having no thoughts, that is an absence of the capacity to think about the self in relation to an other, can be experienced as life lacking any meaning, or attributing a lack of meaning to life; and without meaning life lacks feeling and then there is a sense that life has no purpose. Britton suggests three spheres where precursors of thought, beta elements, might go if they leave the mind: "first into the body; second into the perceptual sphere; and, third into the realm of action—in other words into psychosomatic dysfunction, perceptual hallucination or symptomatic action" (Britton, 1998b, p. 22).

The skin, the membrane that separates inner from outer, takes on a further function as it enables the infant to close its mind to thought and concentrate rather on the disturbances of the body, sometimes self inflicted, ritualized, or experienced as chaotic eruptions, of eczema, asthma, and other somatic disturbances.

> Thus, in later life, psychic pain and mental conflict arising from inner or outer stress are not recognized at the level of verbal thought and discharged through psychic expressions such as dreaming, daydreaming, thinking, or other forms of mental activity; rather they may lead to psychotic solutions of an hallucinatory kind or find discharge in psychosomatic manifestations, as in early infancy. [McDougal, 1989, p. 43]

In some adult patients there is a preoccupation with whole-body activity. The obsessive journey to the gym, the morning routine of frenetic swimming, holds the body and clears the mind. These patients are holding on to their bodies and needing bodily sensation to put them in touch with a feeling of being held and soothed by and within their own skin. Other activities, skiing, diving, and dancing, often activities begun in childhood, may become rigid and necessary defences against the idea of bodily disintegration. They are held onto in a rigid, fixed manner much as some infants may cling vice-like onto hard toys or can only be lulled by constant noise into sleep, thereby bypassing the space in which the body holds the self and an attempt is made to avoid the experience of being alone. This is of course a paradoxical state as the defences create a closed circuit that becomes harder to penetrate and invariably the self becomes increasingly isolated.

Links with psychotherapeutic work

I want now to pull these threads and ideas together and to suggest how this way of thinking can inform psychotherapeutic work. I am saying that if a patient has not experienced himself as being held in the mind of the mother enough to feel a deep mind to mind connection, a series of defences will be erected to protect himself from feeling abandoned. These defences will vary, but the ones I am describing and which seem to come more often into the consulting room are the ones in which a false self is erected to defend the true self against being found. I am suggesting that alongside this false self two other disturbances occur and are linked. A false self cannot afford to think, and thinking has to be defended against because it is painful. Thinking may expose the true self. One way not to think is to fill the mind with ideas and thoughts about the body. The body is experienced as split off from the mind and therefore able to contain ideas that are not linked to thinking.

Bodily sensation, preoccupation with bodily states, food and feeding can distract and soothe and in the therapeutic space it is difficult to find a moment in which a two-person relationship can be thought about. All these non-thoughts, chunterings, ruminations, obsessive calorie-counting or planning and bingeing are in place of working through, and dealing with, painful thoughts about being in mother's mind, and being psychically held and experienced as being real and having a value. Life is experienced as being limited, so that to deny the obsession or preoccupation is experienced by the patient as a threat to their very existence. What will I think of when I cannot think of this that is constantly in my thoughts?

The therapeutic task becomes focused on the relationship between the patient and the therapist, as mostly it is, but the emphasis on the transference and counter-transference is on the capacity to be able to believe and experience that two minds can work together. There has to be real thinking about the self in relation to an other; there has to be a place where memory has meaning and authentic gesture and thought is highly valued. A patient deprived of feeling that he was of particular value to his mother, just one of three children, found that he could not relate to his own children with feeling except when he saw their photographs. When going to a school play he said "all the other parents looked as if they had a buttercup held under their chins, they were beaming, I felt so left out." As he has become able to think that he is of value and that I experience him as authentic and perhaps different from other patients, he has developed a lively sense of connection to his children that he has not before experienced, and the reward for us both is great. He has stopped filling his mind with empty phantasies about being valued for being a false hero and can now begin see the world around him. He is moving slowly out of the conventional trappings of his exaggerated false self. "As the true self is inhibited, I think we can often find in the ordinary exchange of things an extroversion of the false self. That is as the person unconsciously forecloses the spontaneous gesture, he or she exchanges the loss of spontaneity for a gain in false-self exhibitionism" (Bollas, 1995, p. 11). The same patient remembers that in periods such as Christmas where there may have been some thoughts of an exciting kind there were none. In their place he remembers vividly, now in the consulting room, an aching in his legs. This rigidity in his limbs was an attempt to hold onto his body—in so doing he was ensuring that the forbidden thoughts, excitement, disappointments, the richness of life lived would not enter his mind. Another patient rigid in mind and held by the body so rigidly into adulthood that he spent years learning how to relax his muscles and walk with a free gait found that spontaneity first came to him in the smallest exchanges, buying a newspaper, or talking for a moment to a stranger. These acknowledgements that he had a self and could meet others sustained him and gave him his first imaginative glimpse that others had minds and thoughts to which he could link.

REFERENCES

Agger, E. M. (1988). Psychoanalytic perspectives on sibling relationships. *Psychoanalytic Inquiry, 8*: 3–30.

Alvarez, A. (1992). *Live Company: Psychoanalytic Psychotherapy with Autistic, Borderline and Abused Children*. London: Routledge.

Bank, P. B., & Kahn, M. D. (1997). *The Sibling Bond*. New York: Basic Books.

Bion, W. R. (1962a). *Learning from Experience*. New York: Jason Aronson.

Bion, W. R. (1962b). *Learning from Experience*. London: Maresfield.

Bion, W. R. (1967a). The imaginary twin. In: *Second Thoughts* (pp. 3–22). New York: Jason Aronson.

Bion, W. R. (1967b). *Second Thoughts*. London: Maresfield.

Bion, W. R. (1970). *Attention and Interpretation*. London: Tavistock Publications.

Blake, W. (1977). *The Complete Poems*. London: Penguin.

Bollas, C. (1995). *Cracking Up: The Work of Unconscious Experience*. London: Routledge.

Brazelton, T. B. (1969). *Mothers and Infants*. New York: Delta Books.

Britton, R. (1998a). *Belief and Imagination*. London: Routledge.

Britton, R. (1998b). *Belief and Imagination: Explorations in Psychoanalysis*, The New Library of Psychoanalysis 31. London: Routledge.

Britton, R. (1989). The missing link: parental sexuality in the Oedipus

104   REFERENCES

Complex. In: J. Steiner (Ed.), *The Oedipus Complex Today* (pp. 83–102). London: Karnac.

Britton, R. (2000). *What part does narcissism play in narcissistic disorders?* Conference Paper at the Rosenfeld Conference, 18 April 2000.

Byatt, A. S. (1992). *Angels and Insects*. London: Vintage Books.

Case, B. J. (1993). *Living Without Your Twin*. Portland, Oregon: Tibbutt.

Chesterton, G. K. (1999). *Orthodoxy*. London: Hodder and Stoughton.

Colonna, A. B., & Newman, L. M. (1983). The psychoanalytic literature on siblings. *Psychoanalytic Study of the Child, 38*: 285–309.

Dunn, J., & Kendrick, C. (1979). Interaction between young siblings in the context of family relationships. In: M. Lewis & A. Rosenblum (Eds.), *The Child and Its Family* (pp. 143–168). New York: Plenum.

Eliot, G. (1994). *Middlemarch*. London: Penguin.

Eliot, T. S. (1944). Little Gidding. In: *Four Quartets*. London: Faber & Faber.

Engel, G. L. (1975). The death of a twin: mourning and anniversary reactions. Fragments of 10 years self-analysis. *International Journal of Psychoanalysis, 56*: 23–40.

Fleisher, M. L. (1990). Twin fantasies, bisexuality and creativity. *International Review of Psychoanalysis, 17*: 287–298.

Fonagy, P. (1991). Thinking about thinking: some clinical and theoretical considerations in the treatment of a borderline patient. *The International Journal of Psycho-Analysis, 72*: 639–655.

Freud, A. (1936). *The Ego and the Mechanisms of Defence*. Hogarth Press.

Freud, A., & Dann, S. (1951). An experiment in upbringing. *Psychoanalytic Study of the Child, 6*: 127–229.

Freud, S. (1900). *The Interpretation of Dreams*. S.E., 4 & 5.

Freud, S. (1914). *Some Reflections on Schoolboy Psychology*. S.E., 13.

Freud, S. (1916–1917). *Introductory Lectures on Psychoanalysis*. S.E., 15 & 16.

Freud, S. (1923). *The Ego and the Id*. S.E., 19.

Glasser, M. (1985). Some aspects of aggression in the perversions. In: I. Rosen (Ed.), *Sexual Deviation* (2nd ed.) (pp. 278–306). Oxford: Oxford University Press.

Glenn, J. (1966). Opposite sex twins. *Journal of the American Psychoanalytic Association, 14*: 627–657.

Graham, I. (1988). The sibling and its transferences: alternate organisers of the middle field. *Psychoanalytic Inquiry, 8*: 88–107.

Harris Williams, M., & Waddell, M. (1991). *The Chamber of Maiden Thought: Literary Origins of the Psychoanalytic Model of the Mind*. London: Routledge.

Jennings, E. (1986). *Collected Poems*. Manchester: Carcanet.

Joseph, B. (1989). Addiction to near death. In: M. Feldman & E. Spillius Bott (Eds.), *Psychic Equilibrium and Psychic Change: Selected Papers of Betty Joseph* (pp. 127–138). The New Library of Psychoanalysis 9. London: Routledge.

Kernberg, O. (1975). *Borderline Conditions and Pathological Narcissism*. New York: Jason Aronson.

Klein, M. (1957). *Envy and Gratitude*. In: *The Writings of Melanie Klein, Volume 3, Envy and Gratitude and other Works*. London: Hogarth Press.

Klein, M. (1963). On the sense of loneliness. In: R. Money-Kyrle (Ed.), *Envy and Gratitude and Other Works* (pp. 300–313). London: Hogarth Press, 1980.

Klein, M. (1975). *The Psycho-Analysis of Children*. New York: Delta Books.

Kohon, G. (Ed.) (1999). *The Dead Mother: The Work of André Green*. The New Library of Psychoanalysis, 36. London: Routledge.

Kohut, H. (1971). *The Analysis of the Self*. New York: International Universities Press.

Kohut, H. (1984). *How Does Analysis Cure?* Chicago: University of Chicago Press.

Kris, M., & Ritvo, S. (1983). Parents and siblings. *Psychoanalytic Study of the Child, 38*: 311–324.

Lamb, M. E. (1978a). Interactions between eighteen-month-olds and their pre-school-aged siblings. *Child Development, 49*: 51–59.

Lamb, M. E. (1978b). The development of sibling relationships in infancy. *Child Development, 49*: 1189–1196.

Leichtman, M. (1985). The influence of an older sibling on the separation-individuation process. *Psychoanalytic Study of the Child, 40*: 111–161.

Lesser, R. (1978). Sibling transference and counter-transference. *Journal of the American Academy of Psychoanalysis, 6*(1): 37–49.

Lewin, V. (1994). Working with a twin: implications for the transference. *British Journal of Psychotherapy, 10*: 499–510.

McDougall, J. (1989). *Theatres of the Body: A Psychoanalytic Approach to Psychosomatic Illness*. London: Free Association Books.

Meltzer, D. (1966). The relation of anal masturbation to projective identification. *International Journal of Psychoanalysis, 47*: 335–342.

Money-Kyrle, R. (1971). The aim of psycho-analysis. In: D. Meltzer (Ed.), *The Collected Papers of Roger Money-Kyrle* (pp. 442–449). Perthshire: Clunie Press, 1978.

Neubauer, P. B. (1982). Rivalry, envy and jealousy. *Psychoanalytic Study of the Child*, 37: 121–143.

Neubauer, P. B. (1983). The importance of the sibling experience. *Psychoanalytic Study of the Child*, 38: 325–336.

Nissen, B. (2000). Hypochondria: a tentative approach. *International Journal of Psychoanalysis*, 81: 651–666.

Ogden, T. H. (1994). *Subjects of Analysis*. London: Karnac Books.

Parens, H. (1972). Indices of the child's earliest attachment to the mother, applicable in routine pediatric examination. *Pediatrics*, 49: 600–603.

Parens, H. (1979). *The Development of Aggression in Early Childhood*. New York: Jason Aronson.

Parens, H. (1988). Siblings in early childhood: some direct observational findings. *Psychoanalytic Inquiry*, 8: 31–50.

Phillips, A. (1993). *On Kissing, Tickling and Being Bored*. London: Faber and Faber.

Piontelli, A. (1992). *An Observational and Psychoanalytic Study*. London: Tavistock/Routledge.

Province, S., & Solnit, A. J. (1983). Development promoting aspects of the sibling experience. *Psychoanalytic Study of the Child*, 38: 337–351.

Quinodoz, J.-M. (1993). *The Taming of Solitude. Separation Anxiety in Psychoanalysis*. London: Routledge.

Rollman Branch, R. S. (1966). The first born child. *International Journal of Psychoanalysis*, 47: 404–414.

Rosenfeld, H. (1987). Destructive narcissism and the death instinct. In: *Impasse and Interpretation*. Tavistock [Reprinted by Routledge, 1990].

Rudintsky, P. L. (1987). Redefining the revenant; guilt and sibling loss in Gunrip and Freud. *Psychoanalytic Study of the Child*, 43: 423–433.

Sharpe, S. A., & Rosenblatt, A. D. (1994). Oedipal sibling triangles. *Journal of the American Psychoanalytic Association*, 42: 491–523.

Sheerin, D. F. (1991). Fundamental considerations in the psychotherapy of an identical twin. *British Journal of Psychotherapy*, 8: 13–25.

Steiner, J. (1990). Pathological organizations as obstacles to mourning: the role of unbearable guilt. *International Journal of Psycho-analysis*, 71: 87–94.

Steiner, J. (1992). The equilibrium between the paranoid–schizoid and depressive positions. In: R. Anderson (Ed.), *Clinical Lectures on Klein and Bion*. London: Routledge.

Steiner, J. (1993). *Psychic Retreats. Pathological Organizations in Psychotic, Neurotic and Borderline Patients*. London: Routledge.

Wallace, M. (1996). *The Silent Twins*. London: Vintage.

Winnicott, D. W. (1965). *The Maturational Process and the Facilitating Environment: Studies in the Theory of Emotional Development*. London: Hogarth Press.

Winnicott, D. W. (1974). Fear of breakdown. *International Review of Psychoanalysis*, 1: 103–107.

Winnicott, D. W. (1980). *Playing and Reality*. London: Penguin.

Wright, L. (1998). *Twins. Genes, Environment and the Mystery of Identity*. Great Britain: Phoenix.

INDEX